D0891538

IKE'S LETTERS TO A FRIEND

Ike's Letters to a Friend 1941–1958

Edited
with Introduction and Notes by
ROBERT GRIFFITH

UNIVERSITY PRESS OF KANSAS

Published by the University Press of Kansas
(Lawrence, Kansas 66045), which was organized by
the Kansas Board of Regents and is operated
and funded by Emporia State University, Fort
Hays State University, Kansas State University,
Pittsburg State University, the University of
Kansas, and Wichita State University

Library of Congress Cataloging in Publication Data

Eisenhower, Dwight D. (Dwight David), 1890–1969.
Ike's letters to a friend, 1941–1958.

Letters written to Everett Hazlett.
Bibliography: p.
Includes index.
1. Eisenhower, Dwight D. (Dwight David), 1890–1969.
2. Hazlett, Everett E., d. 1958.
3. Presidents—United States—Correspondence.
I. Hazlett, Everett E., d. 1958.
II. Griffith, Robert, 1940–
III. Title.
E836.A4   1984   973.921'092'4   84-13143
ISBN 0-7006-0257-7

Printed in the United States of America

FOR MY COLLEAGUES AND STUDENTS AT THE
UNIVERSITY OF MASSACHUSETTS, AMHERST

Contents

List of Illustrations

Preface

In 1978, while researching a book on post–World War II politics at the Dwight D. Eisenhower Library in Abilene, Kansas, I came across a fascinating exchange of letters between Eisenhower and an old boyhood friend, Everett E. ("Swede") Hazlett. The letters had been open to scholars for only a few years, and few historians had examined them or cited them in their books. I remember thinking at the time how interesting it would be to edit them for publication, and in fact, I returned home with a thick stack of xeroxed copies. In the years that followed, I drew heavily on the Eisenhower-Hazlett correspondence in my own work, especially in a long article entitled "Dwight D. Eisenhower and the Corporate Commonwealth," which appeared in the *American Historical Review* (February 1982); and when the University Press of Kansas indicated an interest in publishing the letters, I naturally leapt at the opportunity.

The letters are located in one of the Eisenhower Library's most important collections, the so-called Ann Whitman file, which was maintained by Eisenhower's private secretary and which contains the nearly quarter of a million documents that received his closest attention. The correspondence consists of more than 150 letters exchanged between the two men between 1941 and 1958. They had occasionally written to one another before 1941, but none of these early letters seem to have survived. Almost all of the existing correspondence is open to the public. The only exception to this is a brief passage in Eisenhower's letter to Swede on 18 November 1957, which remains closed in accordance with restrictions placed upon the collection by the Eisenhower family, and in keeping with a recommendation by the National Security Council to the effect that the release of this material could constitute an unwarranted invasion of the privacy of a foreign citizen. Although a few of Eisenhower's letters to Hazlett have been previously published in the authoritative multivolume *Papers of Dwight D. Eisenhower*, whose nine volumes carry the future president from the beginning of World War II through 1947, the great majority of them appear here for the first time.

Most of Eisenhower's letters appear to have been dictated, not written, a fact that may help to explain occasional awkward phrasings, as well as lapses in grammar and syntax. In editing the letters, I have tried to be as unobtrusive as possible, occasionally using brackets to more fully identify people whose names are mentioned or quietly correcting more or less obvious typographical errors. I have attempted to place each letter in its historical context through headnotes, but have tried to keep footnotes and other scholarly encumbrances to an absolute minimum. For the most part, I have tried to let Eisenhower and Swede tell their own story.

Scholarship is almost always a collective enterprise, and in the preparation of this collection I have accumulated more than a few obligations. I owe a very special debt of gratitude to Dr. John E. Wickman and the fine staff of the Dwight D. Eisenhower Library, without whose assistance this project would never have been possible. Thomas Branigar, an Eisenhower Library archivist and volunteer at the Dickinson County Historical Society, was also helpful in providing information about Abilene and its citizens. I would especially like to thank Burton I. Kaufman and others who read and commented on the manuscript; the American Philosophical Society, which helped make possible my original trip to Abilene; Mrs. Barbara Einfurer and the staff of the University of Massachusetts History Department; and, as always, my family— Barbara, Matthew, and Jonathan. Finally, I would like to affectionately dedicate this volume to my colleagues at the University of Massachusetts, most of whom never "liked Ike," and to my students, almost none of whom are old enough to remember him.

Robert Griffith

Amherst, Massachusetts
March 1984

Introduction

The letters that fill this volume are the product of a friendship between two young men—Everett E. Hazlett ("Swede," the boys called him) and Dwight D. Eisenhower (like several of his brothers, nicknamed "Ike"). Forged during the hot Kansas summer of 1910, their friendship lasted a lifetime—through thirty years during which their lives roughly paralleled one another, and for nearly two decades more during which their lives sharply diverged. Yet the letters that they exchanged are more than simply the chronicle of a friendship; they constitute, as well, a unique self-portrait of one of modern America's most important leaders and a highly revealing inner history of his presidency. "Our deep friendship endured to the day of his death in 1958," Eisenhower later wrote. "Our correspondence over those forty-odd years would fill a thick volume. I drew on it for *The White House Years* because Swede Hazlett was one of the people to whom I opened up."[1]

The story of Ike and Swede begins in Abilene, Kansas, which, despite its brief and lurid history as a Wild West cattle town, was by the time of their youth a sedate midwestern farm community. It was a good place to grow up in, both later recalled, though neither of them returned with any great frequency, and with the passage of years, their ties to the town grew increasingly tenuous.

Nor did they grow up together. Eisenhower, whose father was an "engineer" (*read* mechanic) at the Belle Springs Creamery, lived with his parents and five brothers in a small two-story frame house on the south (and "wrong") side of the railroad tracks. Swede, whose father was a physician and pharmacist, lived with his parents and sister on the more affluent north side of town. Though Swede would later proclaim in a burst of patriotism that "there was never any difference between 'north of the tracks' and 'south

1

Left, Ike in the United States Military Academy's yearbook for 1915; right, Swede in the United States Naval Academy's yearbook for 1915 (courtesy of the Dwight D. Eisenhower Library). "As you well know, it was only through you that I ever heard of the Government Academies. To the fact that you were well acquainted with the methods for entering the Academies and my good fortune that you were my friend, I owe a lifetime of real enjoyment and interesting work" (Eisenhower to Hazlett, 11 October 1941).

of the tracks,'" he was wrong. The lines of class in Abilene, though not impermeable, were clearly drawn and reflected in dozens of subtle and sometimes not so subtle ways. On the south side, where Eisenhower lived, were the small frame houses of the working class. On the north side, where the business and professional classes lived, were many large Victorian homes. As a boy, Eisenhower attended Lincoln Grammar School on the south side, while Swede went to the newer and more modern Garfield School on the north side. It was not until the seventh grade that the kids from "south of the tracks" joined the others at Garfield, an event that was often accompanied by fistfights and other youthful rivalries. Indeed, Ike's two-hour battle with northsider Wesley Merrifield quickly became a town legend.[2]

Nevertheless, when Hazlett arrived at Abilene High School for the beginning of his freshman year, it was Eisenhower who affectionately dubbed him "Swede" and took him under his wing. A sophomore, Eisenhower was already a football star and school hero. Swede, on the other hand, was a gangly blond-headed youth who sometimes became the target of school bullies. "He was a big fellow, too, but he had been raised in a quiet atmosphere and occasionally a few people smaller than he would try to bulldoze him," Ike later recalled. "I felt protective, a sort of obligation to him, and I took it upon myself to tell a few of the so-and-so's to lay off."[3]

Swede spent only a year at Abilene High, however; he completed his high-school education at a military academy in Wisconsin and then secured a congressional appointment to the United States Naval Academy. He failed the mathematics section of the entrance test, however, and came back to Abilene in 1910 to prepare for a reexamination. By the time he returned, Eisenhower had already graduated and was working nights at the creamery. "I had been seeing more and more of Ike, during vacations, as the years went on," Swede recalled, "and this summer I spent many of my evenings at the creamery, helping him to while away the hours. We played a bit of penny-ante poker—giving him the start that ended in his reputation as the best stud player in the Army. Still being kids, more or less, we also weren't above raiding the company's refrigerating room occasionally—for ice cream, and for cold storage eggs and chickens which were cooked on a well-scrubbed shovel in the boiler room."[4]

Before long, Swede had convinced Eisenhower that he, too, should try to secure an appointment to Annapolis. It was not difficult. With one of his older brothers in college at the University of Michigan, and with younger brothers Earl and Milton coming along, Eisenhower found the service academy's free education extremely attractive. As it turned out, he was forced to settle for West Point instead, since he would be twenty-one before the next class enlisted and thus would be too old to begin at Annapolis. Both Ike and Swede passed their entrance examinations the following year and entered their respective schools as members of the class of 1915.

They saw one another only occasionally during their academy years, and even more infrequently after graduating. They wrote from time to time, and though no letters from these years apparently survive, Swede later remembered that during World War I, Eisenhower had written "griping because I was overseas while he was kept at home, training our new tank corps." The two were reunited in 1923, when Ike was stationed at Camp Gaillard in the Panama Canal Zone and the submarine that Swede commanded put in for repairs at the naval base at Coco Solo. Swede was impressed by the fact that Eisenhower had "fitted up the 2nd story screened porch of their quarters as a rough study, and here, with drawing board and texts, he put in his spare time re-fighting the campaigns of the old masters." Eisenhower himself later recalled his tour of duty in Panama, under Gen. Fox Conner, as "a sort of graduate school in military affairs and the humanities." He would later excel at the army's prestigious Command and General Staff School at Fort Leavenworth, Kansas.

Their paths did not cross again until 1935 in Washington, where Ike was serving as a senior aide to Army Chief of Staff Gen. Douglas MacArthur and where Swede, now a commander, was serving in the Navy Department. Swede later recalled that Eisenhower was already "rapidly becoming known as an Army 'comer' . . . but [that] he was still a Major with no immediate prospects." A few months later a reluctant Eisenhower left for the Philippines with MacArthur, and more than a decade elapsed before the two friends would see one another again.

During the years that followed, the lives of both men changed dramatically. In Swede's case, the change was for the worse. A severe heart attack brought his promising career to an end in 1939, on the very eve of World War II. He returned to duty during the war, first as an academic administrator at the naval academy, then later as commander of the naval training program at the University of North Carolina. He retired in 1946, remaining in Chapel Hill with his wife, Elizabeth, or "Ibby" as she was called, and their two daughters, Mary Elizabeth and Alice. He continued to experience poor health, including high blood pressure and excruciating headaches, a second heart attack in 1953, and finally cancer, from which he died in 1958.

Eisenhower, meanwhile, after a sometimes frustrating three years in the Philippines, returned to the United States in 1939 to begin the quick march that would soon lead to his appointment as supreme commander of the Allied Expeditionary Force in Europe and, eventually, to the presidency of the United States.

The correspondence between Eisenhower and Hazlett resumed during the fall of 1941, only a few months before Pearl Harbor. At first, Ike's letters to Swede were short and infrequent, a fact possibly dictated by the heavy demands of command, by wartime censorship, and by Swede's reluctance to intrude on his old friend. There is a tentative quality to these early letters—as though the two men were attempting not only to remember who they had been but also to come to terms with who they had become, trying, as it were, to reestablish a relationship that had been attenuated by the passage of years. In the second of the letters, for example, Ike refers to "Mrs. Hazlett," scarcely a sign of close friendship. In the years that followed, however, the letters increased in length, frequency, and personal warmth. Ike wrote to Swede four or five times a year throughout the late forties and early fifties, and even more often during the presidential years. Nor were his letters perfunctory or merely social; indeed, they increasingly became long and detailed expositions of what Eisenhower was thinking and doing. It is this quality, of course, which makes the collection so interesting to historians.

Though Eisenhower saw Swede only infrequently—on two occasions in 1947, when he was in North Carolina; in 1957, at the second inaugural, and twice while Swede was hospitalized in Bethesda Naval Hospital near Washington—their friendship steadily deepened. For his part, Eisenhower gratefully recalled the pivotal role that Swede had played in the summer of 1910. "As you well know," he wrote in the first of these letters, "it was only through you that I ever heard of the Government Academies. To the fact that you were well acquainted with the methods for entering the Academies and my good fortune that you were my friend, I owe a lifetime of real enjoyment and interesting work." On Swede's part there was tremendous pride in Eisenhower's achievements, as well perhaps as the vicarious satisfaction of those needs that were denied to him in his own career. "I can't begin to tell you what a glow of pleasure I get out of all the honors being heaped upon you," wrote Swede in 1943. But there were also undercurrents of uneasiness in the relationship, especially as Eisenhower became not merely a highly successful army officer but also a national and world hero. These undercurrents were reflected both in Swede's sometimes extravagant praise for Eisenhower and in his sensitivity about the nature of their relationship. "A year ago," Swede wrote in June 1945, "I boasted to all who would listen

5

of our friendship; but now the aura of your glory has become so blinding that I fear even to admit acquaintanceship for fear I'll be accused of 'basking'—something I've never done in my life.'' Ike was quick to respond to Swede's feelings, repeatedly reassuring him that success had not altered their relationship and that he would be upset "if you feel it necessary to say that you didn't know that other guy from Abilene.'' In November 1945 he wrote to Swede that he would "admit, for the sake of argument, (though without acknowledging any sense in the proposition) that so far as the headlines of the past few years are concerned, we are somewhat like Mutt and Jeff. I've been long; you've been short. You will remember that as between Mutt and Jeff themselves, comparative elongation made little difference, either in their recurring fights or in those instances when they were both on the same side of a question. What I am getting at is, so far as the Swede-Ike relationship is concerned, there is no 'big' and certainly no 'little' shot.''

Although Eisenhower, as we have seen, later recalled that Swede was one of the few people to whom he "opened up,'' this is a very relative judgment. Certainly, in the correspondence there is little of an intimate or highly personal nature. Eisenhower didn't "open up,'' in *that* sense, to anyone. He once wrote to a friend: "Anglo-saxon men usually find it difficult to exchange direct expressions of sentiment and affection. I am as subject to this inhibition as is any other person."[5] There was, moreover, an element of circumspection in virtually all of Eisenhower's letters, including those to Swede. In his correspondence, as in his public utterances, Eisenhower was careful not to criticize others or to put to paper words that might, if revealed, prove embarrassing. Nor were there any of the profanities that frequently peppered his private conversation. Indeed, there was a stiff, almost formal quality to most of his correspondence, even to family and good friends such as Swede.

It nevertheless seems clear that the letters to Swede were important to Eisenhower and that they became more so through the years. Once embarked on a letter, some of which ran as long as eight to nine single-spaced typewritten pages, he would indeed pour out his thoughts and feelings. Nor did he shy away from important or controversial topics—Vietnam, the Middle East, civil rights, defense spending, the problem of who would succeed him as president, all found their way into his letters to Swede. The result is thus a documentary record of considerable value in understanding Eisenhower and in evaluating his presidency.

While contemporary observers praised Eisenhower for ending the Korean War, for restoring a measure of political tranquillity after the hysteria of the McCarthy era, and, negatively, for not dismantling the New Deal welfare state, some of them also charged him with a failure to provide leadership in meeting the difficult new challenges of the postwar world. Many portrayed him as a weak and politically naïve president who, as Walter Lippmann put it, was never willing "to break the eggs that are needed for the omelet." A poll of seventy-five historians, conducted during the early 1960s, rated Eisenhower only twenty-second among American presidents, between Andrew Johnson and Chester A. Arthur.

By the end of the 1960s, however, historians and other intellectuals had begun to change their views, portraying Eisenhower as a more complex, intelligent, and even skillful chief executive.[6] The opening in the late 1970s of important new collections by the Eisenhower Library—among them the Eisenhower-Hazlett correspondence—soon led to a flood of books and articles extending and qualifying this new interpretation.[7]

Much of the early "revisionist" literature seemed limited by the debates of the past: Was Eisenhower an active or passive president? Was he a skilled leader or a bumbler? Was he dominant or subordinate in his relations with powerful advisors such as John Foster Dulles? Some revisionist accounts were suffused with nostalgia for the 1950s, a supposedly golden age of lost innocence and balanced budgets; others sought to use Eisenhower as a foil with which to attack the policies of his successors, emphasizing the differences between him and other postwar presidents and ignoring the many similarities.

The steady accumulation of newer studies on the Eisenhower years, however, now permits historians to proceed beyond the narrow limits of the early "revisionist" literature toward a broader, if also more complex, understanding of Eisenhower and the Eisenhower presidency.

The Eisenhower who emerges in these letters was not a dimwit who, as one particularly nasty barb had it, didn't read much "because it made his lips tired," but was a man of solid intelligence, self-confident, orderly, and disciplined in his mental processes. And although he wrote with little grace or literary flair—his letters were, at best, plain-spoken and, at worst, stiff and rhetorical—he nevertheless generally expressed himself both clearly and coherently.

It should also be clear that the Eisenhower who wrote these letters was no apolitical babe in the woods, Walter Lippmann and others to the contrary notwithstanding. To be sure, Eisenhower went to great lengths to avoid labeling himself a politician and almost always used the words "politics" and "politicians" in a pejorative sense, as when he wrote to Swede in 1943 that he did not "mean to sound like a demagogue or a politician." Eisenhower nevertheless understood politics, especially the managerial politics of large organizations, and he fully enjoyed the exercise of power. He may not have been a "Machiavelli in pinstripes," as some overly enthusiastic revisionists have seemed to suggest; but he was nevertheless an extremely skilled chief executive and, within the limits that he believed to be appropriate for presidential action, a successful political leader.[8]

As I have argued elsewhere, Eisenhower was a product of the organizational revolution that had transformed American culture during the twentieth century.[9] He understood the dynamics of large organizations and extolled their ability "to produce orderliness, which means restriction upon irresponsible human action." Yet, at the same time, he feared the propensity of organized interests—"pressure groups," he generally called them—to pursue their own narrow ends or, worse yet, to impose those ends on the state, turning the government itself into little more than a battleground for class conflict. As he told a Columbia University audience in 1948: "Danger arises from too great a concentration of power in the hands of any individual or group. The power of concentrated finance, the power of selfish pressure groups, the power of any class organized in opposition to the whole—any one of these, when allowed to dominate, is fully capable of destroying individual freedom."

Such conflict, Eisenhower believed, was neither necessary nor inexorable. Class interests were interdependent, not irreconcilable. As he told an audience in 1947: "In our tightly knit economy, all professions and callings . . . have points of contact and areas of common interest. Banker or housewife, farmer, carpenter, soldier—no one of us can live and act without effect on all the others." Eisenhower believed that the role of civic-minded managers like himself was to dampen popular passions, to quietly reconcile group conflict, and to convince business, labor, and agriculture to pursue enlightened long-range goals rather than immediate self-interest.

As the letters to Swede make clear, Eisenhower's vision of a harmonious "corporate commonwealth," and of the role of professional managers in resolving conflict, grew out of his military experiences during World War II and out of the bitter interservice rivalries that followed the end of the war. Indeed, Eisenhower's keen sensitivity to the narrow self-interest of the military services constitutes one of the principal themes of this collection, a theme that links his leadership during World War II, his experiences as army chief of staff in 1946 and 1947, his opposition to increased military spending during the late 1950s, and his warning, in his 1961 farewell address, on the dangers of the "military-industrial-complex."

Eisenhower's vision of a harmonious and orderly society at home was closely paralleled by an almost Wilsonian faith in an interdependent and cooperative world order. Indeed, the two were inextricably linked in his mind; for if the United States did not sustain such an order through liberal foreign aid and trade policies, it would be, as he put it, "doomed to eventual isolation and to the disappearance of our form of government." To Swede he gave a single, "simple" example of the problem that the United States faced: "No other nation is exhausting its irreplaceable resources so rapidly as is ours. Unless we are careful to build up and maintain a great group of international friends ready to trade with us, where do we hope to get all the materials that we will one day need as our rate of consumption continues and accelerates?" America faced, he wrote in his diary, what Marxists called the "contradictions of capitalism," both the conflict among the "capitalist states for the domination of the world's surface" and the conflict "between the advanced, industrialized nations of the world and the dependent masses of backward peoples." Here, too, Eisenhower believed, conflict, though real, was inevitable *only* if nations did not abandon their narrow, selfish rivalries for mutual cooperation.

For Eisenhower, as these letters make clear, France became a metaphor for international short-sightedness through its actions in Europe, Indochina, and North Africa. Yet, as he wrote to Swede, "the fact is . . . that while we get almost disgusted with the picture that France . . . presents, we need only to look at the rest of the world—indeed to ourselves—to see many points of similarity." If the Western nations could only resolve their differences on the basis of the "long-term good of all," Eisenhower believed, then "we could laugh at the other so-called 'contradictions' in our system, and . . . be so secure against the Communist menace that it would gradually dry up and wither away." Thus, abroad, as at home, narrow self-interest had to give way to broad long-range goals, and conflict to cooperation and harmony.

There were, of course, sharp limits to Eisenhower's philosophy, and contradictions in it that he never fully faced, much less resolved. His vision of a "corporate commonwealth" was profoundly conservative, indeed, at points almost antidemocratic. He distrusted popular passions, detested conventional politics, and, as his 22 July 1957 letter to Swede makes clear, had little but contempt for Congress. He was insensitive to the plight of the poor and was slow to respond to the burgeoning crisis of civil rights. He never endorsed the Supreme Court's decision in *Brown* vs. *Board of Education of Topeka, Kansas;* indeed, he privately thought that it was a mistake. And when he was compelled to order federal troops into Little Rock, Arkansas, in 1957, he was careful to couch his actions in terms of defending civil order, not civil rights. As he explained to Swede: "My biggest problem has been to make people see . . . that my main interest is not in the integration or segregation question. My opinion as to the wisdom of the decision or the timeliness of the Supreme Court's decision has nothing to do with the case. . . . If the day comes when we can obey the orders of our Courts only when we personally approve of them, the end of the American system . . . will not be far off."

Committed to a minimalist state and to a political economy in which conflict would be resolved voluntarily through cooperation, self-restraint, and disinterested public service, Eisenhower could do little but fume privately when business leaders refused to exercise the restraint that he believed necessary. "I want to give business an honorable place, but they make crooks out of themselves," he angrily told his secretary. More fundamentally, he never recognized, or if he recognized, he chose to ignore, that by minimizing the role of the state, he implicitly endorsed the power relationships created by the marketplace and thus foreclosed the efforts of workers, farmers, and consumers to redress those relationships through governmental intervention.

Nor, finally, could he resolve similar contradictions in his thinking on international affairs. To be sure, Eisenhower's conduct of foreign policy was characterized by restraint, by a constant effort to balance ends and means, and by a refusal to be stampeded by more precipitate advisors. As Robert Divine has observed: "Nearly all of Eisenhower's foreign policy achievements were negative in nature. He ended the Korean War, he refused to intervene militarily in Indochina, he refrained from involving the United States in the Suez crisis, he avoided war with China over Quemoy and Matsu, he resisted the temptation to force a showdown over Berlin, he stopped exploding nuclear weapons in the atmosphere."[10]

Yet, critics of America's cold-war policies are ill-advised to seek in Eisenhower, as some have done, a counterhero or foil to use against Truman and Kennedy and Johnson. Eisenhower fully shared the conservative, anti-Communist premises that shaped postwar American foreign policy, and when he chose, he could act on those premises with ruthless dispatch. Thus, while he declined to intervene militarily in Indochina, this was a decision produced more by France's refusal to meet American conditions than by any particular aversion to the use of force against social revolutions. As he wrote to Swede, he had been unable to obtain "the conditions under which I felt the United States could properly intervene to protect its own interests." After the French collapse, Eisenhower committed the United States to the support of a client state in Vietnam and to the undermining of the Geneva Agreements, both of which actions would lead directly to an expanded American involvement in the decade that followed. Moreover, many of the "successes" of which he boasted to Swede—Iran and Guatemala, for example—have come back to haunt our own times.

The Eisenhower who emerges from these pages thus bears little resemblance to the bumbling caricature of late 1950s journalism. But neither does he fit the mold of those who in recent years have sought to bend the Eisenhower legacy to their own ends, whether liberal opponents of the Cold War, conservative critics of Democratic fiscal policy, or White House aides seeking to "Eisenhowerize" Ronald Reagan. Eisenhower is, rather, a complex, multidimensional historical figure whom we must study on his own terms if we are to understand fully our recent past. It is my hope that the publication of these letters will contribute, in some small measure, to that understanding.

NOTES

1. Dwight D. Eisenhower, *At Ease: Stories I Tell to Friends* (Garden City, N.Y.: Doubleday & Co., 1967), p. 104. Eisenhower's presidential memoirs, collectively entitled *The White House Years*, were published in two volumes as *Mandate for Change, 1953-1956* and *Waging Peace* (Garden City, N.Y.: Doubleday & Co., 1963, 1965).

2. Hazlett to Eisenhower, 17 June 1945, box 17, Ann Whitman File, Name Series, Dwight D. Eisenhower Library; Kenneth S. Davis, *Soldier of Democracy: A Biography of Dwight Eisenhower* (Garden City, N.Y.: Doubleday, Doran & Co., 1945), pp. 74–78; Eisenhower, *At Ease*, pp. 94–95.

3. Eisenhower, *At Ease*, p. 104.

4. What Swede called his "memoirs of Ike," from which the next several pages are in part drawn, are enclosed in Hazlett to Eisenhower, 23 May 1944, box 17, Ann Whitman File, Name Series, Eisenhower Library.

5. Eisenhower to William R. Robinson, 12 July 1951, box 1, Robinson Papers, Eisenhower Library.

6. See especially the articles by journalists Murray Kempton, Garry Wills, and Richard Rhodes and the full-length studies by Herbert S. Parmet, Peter Lyon, and Charles C. Alexander.

7. See, in particular, the work of Stephen E. Ambrose, Blanche Wiesen Cook, Robert A. Divine, Fred I. Greenstein, Richard H. Immerman, Burton I. Kaufman, Douglas Kinnard, Gary W. Reichard, and Elmo Richardson.

8. For a recent and provocative study of Eisenhower's leadership see Fred I. Greenstein, *The Hidden-Hand Presidency: Eisenhower as Leader* (New York: Basic Books, Inc., 1982).

9. For an elaboration of the themes that follow see Robert Griffith, "Dwight D. Eisenhower and the Corporate Commonwealth," *American Historical Review* 87 (Feb. 1982): 87–122.

10. Robert A. Divine, *Eisenhower and the Cold War* (New York: Oxford University Press, 1981), p. 154.

1941

In 1939, shortly after the beginning of World War II, Eisenhower returned from the Philippines to take up a series of important staff assignments and to begin his meteoric rise through the army's higher ranks. In June 1941 he became chief of staff for the Third Army and was stationed at its headquarters in San Antonio, Texas. In September 1941, just before his fifty-first birthday, he was promoted to the temporary rank of brigadier general. Meanwhile Swede, who had suffered a severe heart attack in 1939, had returned to light duty as a teacher and administrator at the United States Naval Academy. On October 5 he sent Eisenhower a letter of congratulations on his recent promotion. "It gave me as much pleasure," he wrote, "as if the honor had come to myself. For I still feel, you know, somewhat responsible for your having launched yourself in a service career."

Among the old Abilene friends to whom Eisenhower refers in his reply were Charles Harger, the owner and editor of the *Abilene Daily Reflector*, a prominent Abilene Republican who had helped Eisenhower secure his appointment to West Point; Charles A. Case, an attorney and director of the Abilene National Bank; Arthur Hurd, another prominent attorney; Reynold Rogers, a banker; Joner (sometimes Jonah) Callahan, who ran a drugstore; Oscar and William Sterl, who owned a men's clothing store; and John Henry Giles, an Abilene lumber dealer.

11 October 1941

Dear Swede:

Of all the things that have happened to me incidental to my promotion, none has been nicer than the receipt of your very fine letter. I truly appreciate it.

I am happy to know that in spite of the affliction of a defective "pump" you are engaged in work that is not only necessary, but which is an integral part of our effort to re-arm. While it is naturally a disappointment to you that you cannot be taking part in the more strenuous phases of naval activity, it must be a source of great satisfaction to know that you are doing something well that must be done. In the Army our biggest job is the production of young leaders. To it we give more concern than to any other single thing. Anyone who has studied this defense problem seriously will readily see that your job is one of vital, even if indirect, importance to the final solution. On top of all this, you must be developing into a bang-up "prof" when they have already made you the Executive of the department.

Both last summer and this I made very short visits to Abilene. My Father and Mother are both still living there, although both are getting feeble. During each visit, I have had a chance to call on most of our old friends, notably Mr. Harger, Charlie Case, Art Hurd, Reynold Rogers, the Sterl Brothers and Henry Giles. I mustn't forget Joner Callahan. All of them seem to be going their accustomed ways with very little noticeable change either in themselves or in the town.

I will not worry you with a recital of the many various details since I last saw you. However, shortly after coming back from the Philippines, I was again placed on staff duty, and at present am Chief of Staff, Third Army. I scarcely need say that I am kept busy.

My son, John, entered West Point this summer. I think that his deeper affections really attracted him toward Annapolis, but some years ago we discovered in him a slight color confusion with respect to the fainter shades; enough so that we were told he could not meet the Naval Academy requirements in this respect. For some years, his O.A.O. [one and only] has been a young Navy gal named Nancy Sabalot. One of his final acts before entering the Point was to go through Washington to see her once more. He is 6'1", weighs only about 145, and is blond, gangly and awkward. When he fills out he ought to be quite a boy. So far, he is apparently doing well enough in his studies, but is having a terrific time with demerits.

You are quite right in your thought that you are responsible for my being in the Military Service. As you well know, it was only through you that I ever heard of the Government Academies. To the fact that you were well acquainted with the methods for entering the Academies and my good fortune that you were my friend, I owe a lifetime of real enjoyment and interesting work. Incidentally, every time I go home I remind all and sundry of this.

Mamie and I send our very best to you both. I will try to do my part in seeing that our correspondence is not interrupted by another three year lapse.

As ever,

1942

In December 1941, less than a week after Pearl Harbor, Eisenhower was ordered to Washington by Army Chief of Staff George C. Marshall, who quickly assigned him to work on the organization of U.S. and Allied military efforts in the Far East. By early 1942, however, Eisenhower was already looking beyond the immediate crisis and toward the development of a broad strategic concept for conducting the war. On his desk pad he wrote: ''We've got to go to Europe and fight—and we've got to quit wasting resources all over the world and still worse—wasting time. If we're to keep Russia in, save the Middle East, India and Burma; we've got to begin slugging with air at Western Europe; to be followed by a land attack as soon as possible.'' Planning for this operation, which was approved by President Roosevelt in April and given the code name BOLERO, would occupy virtually all of Eisenhower's time and energy in the ensuing months. In May he flew to London to confer with the British Chiefs of Staff on the critical issue of a unified command. He returned to the War Department on June 3, the same day on which he wrote the following brief note to Swede. A week later, Marshall named Eisenhower commanding general for the European Theater of Operations, and on June 23 he left for London once again.

3 June 1942

Dear Swede:

My excuse for not answering earlier your nice invitation of May 21 is that I have been out of the country. I just returned this morning and find that Mamie has been up at West Point and will return this evening or tomorrow.

I am sorry to have missed the ball-game, but I expect to take most seriously your invitation to come to Annapolis for a weekend. Just when that can be, the Lord only knows, but it would be a real pleasure to spend a quiet time with you and Mrs. Hazlett.

I hope it won't be long before I can send you a warning note that we will be on the way unless you stop us.

Thank you a lot for your congratulations and good wishes. I am not sure that the congratulations are deserved, but the good wishes are certainly needed!

Cordially,

1943

Almost a year passed before the two friends again exchanged letters. In the intervening months the plans of Eisenhower and other American leaders for a cross-Channel invasion of France had been delayed as the Allies struck instead in North Africa. Eisenhower was named commander in chief of the combined operation and was promoted to the rank of general, receiving his fourth star in February 1943. By April, and in spite of a host of military and political complications, the campaign was nearing its successful completion.

7 April 1943

Dear Swede:

You cannot imagine how much good your letter did me. It arrived two days ago and already I have read it three times. I have received lots of proforma congratulations, but no other letter has seemed to me to be so genuine in its expression of good will and in its appreciation of the fact that all the hardest tests are yet to come.

Nothing that I can say can possibly ease your disappointment in being excluded from the more active phases of this war effort. However, as the responsibilities thrust upon me have become wider and heavier, I have come to appreciate more and more clearly how true it is that nations, not armies and navies, make war. Everybody has a job. Yours happens to be in a niche that does not completely satisfy all the training you have received, the experience you have gained, and the thought you have expended in the naval profession. But I am almost fanatic in my belief that only as we pull together, each of us in the job given him, are we going to defend and sustain the priceless things for which we are fighting. It seems to me that in no other war in history has the issue been so distinctly drawn between the forces of arbitrary oppression on the one side and, on the other, those conceptions of individual liberty, freedom and dignity, under which we have been raised in our great Democracy.

I do not mean to sound like a demagogue nor a politician. In fact, once this war is won, I hope never again to hear the word "politics." But I do have the feeling of a crusader in this war and every time I write a letter or open my mouth, I preach the doctrine that I have so inadequately expressed above.

Needless to say, it would be a great pleasure to have you by my side. Admiral [Ernest J.] King gave me a Naval Reserve officer (Lt. Comdr. [Harry C.] Butcher) for a Naval Aide. He lives with me and is my constant companion. All other naval officers in this command are incorporated in the navy set-up, the Americans under Vice Admiral [H. Kent] Hewitt, who reports in turn to Admiral of the Fleet [Sir Andrew Browne] Cunningham (one of the finest men I have had the privilege of meeting).

Thanks again for your fine letter. I hope that when this war is over, you and I can get together to review events and relate to each other our experiences.

With cordial regard,

As ever,

After the victory in North Africa, Eisenhower turned his attention to Italy, where Allied forces under his command landed first in Sicily and then, in September 1943, on the toe of the boot itself. By early October the Allies had taken Naples; but the advance then stalled as the Germans committed some twenty-five divisions to the defense of Italy while the Allies, at the same time, began diverting troops and supplies for a long-delayed cross-Channel invasion of France.

---

20 October 1943

Dear Swede:

Your letters are not only entertaining; they are fine for my ego. Naturally, I like to get them.

I can well understand your disappointment in being turned down again by the medicos. However, I am happy to see that you have taken the decision as philosophically as is possible and are not letting it get you down. In a way, your case is like that of [my brother] Milton's. He thoroughly detested his final job in Washington but felt that it was most essential to the war effort and felt rather guilty in considering the acceptance of the presidency of Kansas State. He cabled me on the matter and I sent him a long message, setting forth my own ideas in considerable detail. Briefly, they are that no man in the world today has a more responsible job than those who are influencing the thinking of the younger generation, yet in school. The teaching of the obligations as well as the privileges of American citizenship, the virtue of old-fashioned patriotism, the need for a clean, honest approach to intricate problems and the necessity for earnest devotion to duty, are things that must be thoroughly inculcated in the rising generation, if we are to survive as a sturdy nation.

You may say that such a thought provides only cold comfort to a man who is trained for emergency action and, when the emergency arises, is confined to something that is not to his personal liking. I really think you would be wrong in feeling that way. I mingle all the time with men of our armies, men of considerable intelligence. It is amazing to find out how few have any concept of obligation to the country that has given them privileges which they assume to be a God-given right and theirs without cost. It is amazing also to hear ideas expressed which indicate a belief in the invincibility of America, whether or not she really girds up her loins to wage a bitter fight. Therefore, the soldier often sees no reason why he should be undergoing hardship and discomfort, and one of our major problems is to attempt education along these lines at the same time that the man is called upon to enter a fight where strong convictions along such lines would be the surest way of making him invincible on the battlefield.

This is clumsily and possibly even incoherently stated but I am sure you will detect my absolute sincerity.

I am writing to my son John today. Whether or not he will get down toward Annapolis and, if he should, whether or not he could compete, even momentarily, with the snappy blue uniforms of the Midshipmen, I still feel that I owe it to him to pass on your information as to your older daughter. At least they have two things in common—they are both blondes and their fathers are both from Abilene, Kansas.

My very best to you and your family and please write to me when you get a chance.

Cordially,

P.S. In late years I have seen Bob Baughey [Robert M. Baughey, a public-relations officer in the War Department] occasionally and, at one time, I asked him to go along with my command. At that time he had another job in view and so I have lost track of him. However, I will send his name on to the proper Staff Section to determine whether I might get him over here for assignment.

1945

A year and a half elapsed before Eisenhower again wrote to Swede. In the intervening months, of course, Eisenhower had organized and led the Allied invasion of Europe. The story of that effort, which began on 6 June 1944, is among the most often told of the war and need not be repeated here. Suffice it to say that by April 1945, when Eisenhower next wrote to his old friend, Germany's armed forces had been shattered. Eisenhower himself had been awarded a fifth star and had been promoted to the newly created rank of General of the Army. In his letter to Eisenhower on January 29, Swede had expressed a preference for the title of Marshal, but then had observed that the problem created by George C. Marshall's name probably had led to its rejection. He also had written that while he thought that the navy "usually did things better than the Army," he did give the army credit for "dipping deep in the hat and pulling you up to the top when you were needed." At the same time, he wrote, this wasn't "a very flattering commentary on the thousand odd files who outranked you." Swede, meanwhile, had been eased out of the Naval Academy to make room, as he put it, for the "young, be-medaled heroes just back from the wars." He was promoted to captain and placed in charge of the navy's Reserve Office Training Corps program at the University of North Carolina.

18 April 1945

Dear Swede:

Your letter of 29th January took almost three months to reach me—I don't know whether it is because your North Carolina station may be off the main rail lines, or because I have neglected to give my postal authorities the devil for the past several weeks.

I agree with your opinion on the awkwardness of my current title. Luckily, every General in our Army has always been addressed as "General" whether or not he officially has qualifying terminology in front of the word or behind it. You are quite right in observing that it doesn't matter a darn to me.

Nothing in your letter intrigued me more than your comparisons in the Army and Navy systems, as applied to their methods in selecting their field leaders in time of war. You seem to believe the Army was almost foolhardy in the matter but did believe that it took a certain amount of nerve to shatter precedent. Finally, it occurred to you that the Army system is not very flattering to the files that were jumped in the process. With this particular point I do not quite agree. As I see it, seniority, in itself, is of little moment in time of war. The head of the whole organization must make his best guesses as to the individuals he considers equipped for particular tasks and then he perforce gives them the rank suitable to the task. His choice usually falls upon those that he believes will make good—if he makes a wrong guess then he has to correct the mistake. This process applies all the way down the line. Seniority normally means experience, and experience is always important. But endurance and experience are not to be confused in their meaning, and experience alone will never meet the peculiar requirements of war leadership.

This same process applies throughout. Every day we are selecting men here for division or corps command, and our selections normally do not take seniority into account unless all other factors are so nearly equal that this one should govern. In the average case the ranks conferred are for the war only and everybody can go back to his old rank and seniority can again have its heyday.

I am much interested in your new job and sincerely hope that you won't work too hard. It is especially gratifying that you are your own boss and can therefore apply to your job more of your own individual ideas.

Your tale about reactions and conditions at home is highly intriguing. I don't know exactly what it takes to work the United States up to a real fighting pitch and to keep it there, but it is very difficult for us here to believe that anyone can take this thing as a routine affair, and have much time to think of profits, night clubs and horse-racing. Actually, I think that the average American feels much more deeply about these matters than we normally assume. I receive lots of mail and invariably it reflects a very serious attitude.

Not long ago I had a chance to see my son. He was much annoyed with me that I took him away from his job with one of the fighting corps to come back a little ways to see me. However, we had a splendid evening. Since I had not then received your letter I didn't have a chance to remind him that your blonde is still unmarried. Anyway, my love to her and to "Ibby." Incidentally, my curiosity is stirred every time I see that nick-name in one of your letters. What is the legal version?

As ever,

Eisenhower arrived back in the United States in June 1945 for a round of triumphant public appearances. In mid July he returned to Germany as commanding general of United States Forces, European Theater, and commander in chief of United States occupation forces in Germany. For the next six months he was immersed in the almost daily crises of the occupation. Although he handled this new job with his customary skill and patience, it seems clear that his heart was never in it and that like the men and women under his command, he was anxious to have done with the aftermath of the war and to return home. "I must say," he wrote to a former aide, "that the job of fighting a war was not so wearing in its irritations and frustrations as is that of trying to produce peaceful and effective agreements to carry out governmental policies in Central Europe."

Swede, of course, was tremendously proud of his old friend, but he was also a little uneasy about Eisenhower's new celebrity. "A year ago, and for many years before that, I blasted to all who would listen of our friendship," he wrote; "but now the aura of

Eisenhower's triumphant return to Washington, D.C., 18 June 1945 (by permission of United Press International).

your glory has become so blinding that I fear even to admit acquaintanceship for fear I'll be accused of 'basking,'—something I've never done in my life." Somewhat taken aback by Eisenhower's vigorous defense of the army's promotion policies, Swede also apologized for having bothered Eisenhower with the issue at the height of the final offensive against the Germans.

Dear Swede:

Although I talked to you on the phone this morning, I am writing this note because since that hour, I have read the letter you wrote me on the 17th of June. I do not remember exactly what the point was in our "promotion" discussion; but it is possible that I merely felt it necessary to listen to my own voice on the subject. In any event, I assure you I had no feeling that we were in any hot argument. All such subjects as that have a definite fascination for me and I am apt to get very verbose, once I get started.

As for writing you on April 18—if that was the date—I knew on March 24 that the enemy was absolutely whipped and was rapidly disintegrating. He had not the slightest chance and from then on it was merely a question of when could we get either an orderly surrender to all the combined powers, or failing that completely occupy his country. During mid-April my mind was completely at ease so far as the actual fighting was concerned.

I am sorry to note in your letter that you are beginning to find it necessary to play down our lifelong friendship. Making the headlines has a thousand disadvantages, but I am going to be upset if you feel it necessary to say that you didn't know that other guy from Abilene.

I haven't the slightest idea of what is happening or is to happen in the Pacific. I do know that I am not to be officially connected with it in any way. My own admiration for [Adm. Chester W.] Nimitz is probably no less than yours even though I know him only by hearsay and by his accomplishments. Every word I have ever heard about him confirms the feeling that I always get when I look at his picture—he is top flight in every respect.

My best to Elizabeth and please don't wait so darn long before writing to me again.

As ever,

Eisenhower returned to the United states in November 1945 to succeed George Marshall as army chief of staff. For the next two years he would be preoccupied with the army's campaign for Universal Military Training (UMT), with the struggle over military unification, and with the attempt to devise a military strategy for the emerging Cold War. The battle over unification was particularly intense, with the navy strongly resisting efforts to consolidate the three services. A unification bill finally passed Congress, as Title II of the National Security Act of 1947, but not before it had been considerably weakened by naval opposition.

27 November 1945

Dear Swede:

This time your letter caught me in the hospital, flat on my back trying to ward off serious consequences from a very heavy cold and an attack of bronchitis. So for once it doesn't seem worth while to try to convince you that your letters, far from being a bore, are entertaining, interesting and helpful. But with regard to the reluctance you feel in writing to me, I will admit, for the sake of argument, (though without acknowledging any sense in the proposition) that so far as the headlines of the past few years are concerned, we are somewhat like Mutt and Jeff. I've been long; you've been short. You will remember that as between Mutt and Jeff themselves, comparative elongation made little difference, either in their recurring fights or in those instances when they were both on the same side of a question. What I am getting at is, so far as the Swede-Ike relationship is concerned, there is no "big" and certainly no "little" shot. In all sincerity, and with the utmost frankness, your letters present to me a more objective view on the subjects we discuss than any other advice I get. You can well imagine how I look forward to receiving the very few communications you deign to send me.

With all that out of the way, I'll get down to the matter I want to discuss now. As you would guess, it is "unification." You reflect some of the fears I have heard voiced either in the press or verbally by other naval officers, namely, that some "swallowing up" process would inevitably follow upon any closer unification of the Services, at the top, than we now have. Frankly, I not only cannot understand how such a thing could come about—I am certain that no one wants it and I, for one, would battle it to the death. One brother does not devour another; a guard on a football team is equally important with the tackle!

The American public should understand that war has become a triphibious affair, and unless one laboriously picks out special circumstances, land, sea and air in varying ratio are employed in every operation of war. The closest possible kind of association among the individuals of these three forces throughout their Service careers is mandatory. You must remember that for the past three and a half years I have *not* been an infantryman! I have not even been a *ground* commander. I have had land, sea and air, and during that period I believe that my viewpoint has been as much naval and as much air as it has been ground. I do not mean that I've learned the techniques of sea and air; but if my headquarters had not had the sense to give as much weight to the technical advice of those two Services as in the case of ground, then our operation would have failed.

Yet it was a laborious process at the beginning to weld all these three Services together and to convince each, in the field, that its own characteristics, capabilities and welfare would be as influential in determining upon an operation as would those of the other two Services. Early conferences were carried on almost in the "cat-bulldog" atmosphere, each Service fighting for itself and its requirements and quite certain that no one else was concerned in them. This mutual suspicion and fear rapidly melted away and I think there is no question that GHQ, both in the Mediterranean and in Northwest Europe, was almost a model of unified, integrated, and enthusiastic cooperation. But I believe that we should in time of peace so organize and train that a happy family can start operating in this fashion on the day we put it together, not after each Service finds by experience that the others regard it as a friend and part of the team rather than one of the enemies in the operation.

What I have said is not mere loose talk or even merely an impression. It is fact and I could give you a number of instances as specific illustrations. Moreover, the fault was not to be found exclusively with any one Service. However, all this is somewhat beside the point because everybody now agrees that *in any war theater there should be one commander* and his authority should be so clearly established that there is no question as to his right to handle the three Services as he sees fit. The real point at issue is whether or not there would be any peacetime advantage in establishing by law a closer unification at the top.

Now forget for a moment that you are a naval officer and regard yourself merely as a taxpayer. You are interested in national security and therefore in the armed forces of your country. You are entitled to some kind of presentation or explanation that would enable you to make a reasonable guess whether this whole subject is being properly treated by Congress or whether all of the fighting Services are being placed on a starvation basis and their efficiency reduced to former deplorable levels. Since war is a triphibious matter, how can you make any judgment upon this matter at all—whether you are in private life or whether you are chairman of a Congressional Committee—*unless the broad yearly program for all three Services is presented to you as a unit?* Do you not need to know whether ground forces have been provided to complement the navy and the air, and the navy both the others? If the members of each of these Services—and remember that service pride and esprit in each are equally strong—come to you *unilaterally* and plead for support, I am unable to see how you can get a balanced picture. Each of the Services will consider itself individually responsible for the safety of the nation and, if you are truly security minded, you will wind up with numbers of duplications which in the long run you cannot afford. The degree of autonomy that should be permitted to each Service so far as its own operations and its own affairs are concerned, should not be lessened. But all of us get into our heads that no one of these Services is complete within itself—that it needs the other two—and that since each is complementary to the other two, the whole program of preparation must be a balanced one. Added to this it is well to remember that the example of single command would have a great effect upon the second lieutenant and the ensign as well as upon all the men they command.

It seems to me that such a system, also, will provide more easily for combined training and closer association of individuals through the years. On this subject I am almost a fanatic. War is a matter of teamwork, and teamwork is not possible among people that are mutually suspicious. I will put it stronger than this: perfect teamwork can be achieved *only* among friends.

I had not heard that any other person had ever suggested a single uniform, which I did once, merely to illustrate the extent to which I believe we should all think of ourselves as one common family. I do not suggest what that uniform should be, and actually I think it is probably an impracticable suggestion, possibly even an unwise one, but if such a thing were adopted I personally would not care one whit what the color of the uniform should be. It could be blue, green, olive drab or a skyblue pink. On that point, however, I accept your suggestion and will not mention it again!

One other thing I should like to make plain. I think I told you before of my admiration for Nimitz, based upon newspaper accounts and reports of friends, and many of the naval officers with whom I have come in contact in this war. Because it happens that argument on this subject has largely, to my astonishment, developed into an Army-Navy argument, I would very much like to see, if the thing ever comes about, a *naval* officer designated as the first Chief of Staff to the Secretary of the Armed Forces. So far as I am concerned there is not the slightest bit of personal or Service consideration attached to the project. Until a few weeks ago every naval officer I had met was an enthusiastic supporter of the idea. I believed that there would be some argument on the matter, particularly in Congress, but I really thought that the great mass of army and navy officers were for the thing 100%.

For myself, there is nothing I want so much as opportunity to retire. If this evening, as I lie here in bed, I could believe that when I got up I could get Mamie down here from her hospital and we could start out roaming the United States looking for the home we would like to live in the rest of our years, I would be up and on the go within twenty minutes. The job I am taking now represents nothing but straight duty. Naturally I will do it as well as I know how, but I do hope that when I get a chance to meet Nimitz and the rest of the Navy files, I can convince them that no consideration of personal or Service ambition has a single thing to do with my views.

I know of many examples of perfect cooperation and teamwork between armies, navies and ground forces of two nations that would delight your heart to hear. Possibly one day I will try to write them down. They were heart-warming experiences. But the tragedy was that initially, at least, they were considered notable, almost unique. I hold that perfection of teamwork and of friendly cooperation should be accepted as a matter of course and I believe we can bring that about if we practice it and preach it and so organize as to exemplify it in time of peace. We will always have enough esprit de corps in each Service. Continuance of the Army-Navy game will itself insure sufficient competition to make us both want to excel.

You mentioned a number of younger admirals in your letter. Of them I think I know only [Rear Adm. Forrest P.] Sherman. I wish you would ask your brother-in-law [Rear Adm. Frank G. Fahrion] to drop in on me the next time he goes through Washington. I should like very much to see him.

Until you mentioned again the publication of my speeches [Swede had been asked to write a forward to a collection of Eisenhower's speeches, the profits from which were to go to the Army Relief Fund] I had forgotten all about the matter. I will look it up as I had given my permission subject, however, to the proviso that neither the publisher nor myself would make a cent out of the matter. I do not know what has happened.

My best to you and Ibby, and whenever I can get that son of mine home from Germany I will chase him up to Frederick to call on the little "Miss Swede."

Take care of yourself,

Cordially,

1946

Eisenhower and Swede continued to joke about encouraging a romance between their children, John Eisenhower and Mary Elizabeth Hazlett. Swede had earlier asked Eisenhower to remind his son that there was "a damned good-looking (and sensible) blonde out at Hood College at Frederick who would like to meet him."

---

25 January 1946

Dear Swede:

Thank you very much for the copy of the Chapel Hill Weekly. I enjoyed the editorial and the article as well as your note.

The article was particularly amusing so far as I was concerned because it proved that in spite of your laborious efforts to deny acquaintanceship with me someone finally caught up with you.

I probably wrote you in my most recent letter that I personally have nothing further to say on the subject of unification. So far as I am concerned the greatest factor in the problem right now is my conviction that Nimitz is a man of extraordinary qualifications, including ability and devotion to duty, and on top of these, is a friendly soul with whom it is a pleasure to work. He and I communicate constantly and no matter what the outcome should be in Congress I have no doubt that he and I will succeed in instituting a lot of reforms that are badly needed.

My son is still in Germany. In fact, even if he should be ordered to some other duty as a matter of mere routine I would probably have to stop him because there would be an accusation of favoritism. Aside from the natural desire of Mamie and myself to see him, I am hopeful that he will get home and meet that daughter of yours before she goes and gets herself married. I chuckle to myself every time you and I exchange any ideas along this line because the spectacle of a couple of old-time Kansas farmer boys timidly sticking their noses into Cupid's business is, after all, a bit on the ludicrous side.

Love to your family and warm regards to yourself,

As ever,

Even before the war was over, prominent Americans were urging Eisenhower to run for the presidency; and although Eisenhower undoubtedly had at least considered the possibility, he continued to insist throughout his private correspondence, as he did in public, that he had absolutely no such ambition. In October 1945 Swede had written that "no matter what party you affiliated with, (and I have no idea if you're D. or R.) you could carry the country without even taking to the road." The following February, Swede returned to the subject, concluding, however, that "I have an idea that you have no real interest in public office."

Swede, whose health continued to decline, had meanwhile been relieved of his command of the Naval ROTC at North Carolina. Although offered several posts at the university, he declined them, deciding instead to devote himself to retirement and to the occasional writing of juvenile fiction.

---

13 March 1946

Dear Swede:

Thank you very much for your letter which was written while I was on my recent swing around the country. I stopped at Abilene and saw Charlie Harger, Sam Heller [president of the United Trust Company in Abilene] and Charlie Case. Others I didn't get to see because I was too rushed.

I share your sympathy for Bradley.[1] You can be certain that he took that job only because he was ordered to do so. He was under no illusions as to the shower of brickbats that was certain to come his way. However, in that respect his attitude was no different from mine with regard to this post I am occupying.

Your conclusions concerning my attitude toward politics are 100 per cent correct. When trying to express my sentiments myself I merely get so vehement that I grow speechless, if not hysterical. I cannot conceive of any set of circumstances that could ever drag out of me permission to consider me for any political post from Dog Catcher to "Grand High Supreme King of the Universe." Moreover, I find myself in rather general agreement with your general observations concerning the receptive boys.

It was a blow to Beetle Smith when he was told that they wanted him to accept the Moscow job.[2] He is a thorough-going soldier, extremely capable and occupies a place of high regard and esteem among those people in Europe with whom he worked. I know of no one better qualified for the job but of course his ambitions do not lie along diplomatic and political lines.

In the same position I am sure that I would feel the same as you do about taking a job in the University. I would far rather attempt to write. You have a distinct flair in that line and I don't see why even "light fiction" should be beyond your reach. I am certain that there are a number of special writing fields in which

1. Gen. Omar N. Bradley, who had commanded the American forces in the Normandy invasion, served as head of the Veteran's Administration from 1945 to 1947. Swede had written that his heart went out to Bradley and "his enmeshment in [American] Legion politics."

2. Gen. Walter Bedell Smith, who had served as Eisenhower's chief of staff during World War II, had just been named ambassador to the Soviet Union, where he served for the next three years.

you could enter with real success. Anyway it is the type of effort that should be fun and even if the publishers won't take your stuff, I'll bet a nickel that Ibby would like it—possibly even your young blonde. Why don't you start writing some Wild West stories; I guarantee I'll read them. Moreover, I will write to the publishers and demand that I want to read "Wild Bill and the Long-horned Steer," "Early Days in Abilene," "The Smokey Hill,"—all by E. E. Hazlett, Jr. Maybe we can work out a reciprocal agreement. You do the writing, I'll do the reading and I'll howl to every publisher for more and more of your stories.

My love to the family and warm regard to yourself,

As ever,

Eisenhower wrote this letter shortly after a joint task force under the command of the Joint Chiefs of Staff (JCS) had detonated the first of two atomic tests at Bikini atoll in the Pacific. The SHAEF (Supreme Headquarters Allied Expeditionary Forces) Reports that Eisenhower mentions included both his "Report on Operations in Northeast Europe" and a copy of the February 1944 directive to the supreme commander from the Combined Chiefs of Staff. Publication of the reports was designed, at least in part, to answer criticism of the conduct of the European campaigns.

---

1 July 1946

Dear Swede:

I am sorry that your trip had to be put off but please count on staying in our house whatever time you can spend in Washington when you come through this way. We have lots of room in the old house at Fort Myer and you can be as comfortable there as any place else in the City. Certainly, it is about ten degrees cooler than in the center of town.

Right now my plans call for me being out of town between the 15th and 21st of July and between the 1st and 20th of August. Outside of these two periods I expect to be in Washington almost constantly. Between the 10th and 15th of September I will probably have some prominent guests from Britain staying in the house but otherwise the slate is rather clear. If your own plans would so develop that you simply had to go through here during a period when I am absent, then we will have to count on your stopping by on your way back home. Please do not feel anything but the greatest freedom and confidence in coming up to the house; Mamie and I are really looking forward to a visit with you and your family. As an added attraction, I might tell you there is even an elevator in the house so that if the doctors are always jumping you about climbing stairs you can thumb your nose at them.

This morning's papers say that the first test shot at Bikini went off alright. While I am certain that we will learn much from the technical reports, my own idea is that if this hellish contrivance is really effective against ships, it will be from some type of under water use rather than from air bursts. However, we can wait and see.

Because you were interested enough to want to read one of the SHAEF Reports, it occurred to me that you might like to have one in your library. I will get hold of one at once and send it under separate cover. You understand, of course, that it was written a year ago and that I have never had time really to go over it and edit it as I should like. A few of the paragraphs or pages were written personally; the most of it was done by the Historical Section from the records they had in Europe and I got a chance merely to take out most of the vertical pronouns and to insert items that I thought of particular interest. All that was done before I came home last November and I have not since changed it in any way at all. Security staffs went over it—when the Combined Chiefs of Staff agreed to its publication—to make sure that nothing in it violated standing agreements concerning secret matter. No other changes were made.

With warmest regards to you and your family.

As ever,

1947

"You've owed me a letter for damned near a year," wrote Swede on 28 March 1947, quickly adding, however, that "I have no complaints." In any case, Eisenhower and Mamie visited the Hazletts in April during a trip to nearby Fort Bragg. They talked about the presidency, the "burning question," as Swede put it. "I still insist you're the best man in sight and could have it in a walkaway," Swede wrote. "But if you don't want it, that's that!" The following month, Swede sent Eisenhower the original of an illustration that had appeared in the Hearst papers, along with excerpts from Kenneth Davis's biography of Eisenhower.

22 May 1947

Dear Swede:
Instantly on receipt of your letter I looked into the matter of the receipt here of a set of prints of the drawings made by your friend, Mr. William Prince, for Kenneth Davis' book "Soldier of Democracy." I am enclosing a copy of a letter which I sent to Mr. Prince, which, I believe, is self-explanatory. Incidentally, the original drawing of which you wrote was received this morning. I think it is exceptionally good.

Chapel Hill, North Carolina, April 1947 (courtesy of Dwight D. Eisenhower Library). The Eisenhowers visited the Hazletts while Ike was on a tour of duty at nearby Fort Bragg as army chief of staff. They talked about the presidency. "I still insist you're the best man in sight and could have it in a walk-away," wrote Swede. "But if you don't want it, that's that!"

I am due in Raleigh on August 28 to speak at the Farmers' and Farm Women's Convention. I would be delighted to see you, but frankly have no knowledge of how much time I will have available for myself. Customarily when I am the guest, I leave the matter of my entire schedule in the hands of my hosts. However, in this instance, I will ask my aide to get in touch with you about the first of August to see if perchance we can have a few minutes together in my hotel suite at Raleigh, and also to inquire about the possibility of having you attend the dinner at which I shall speak. As far as I know now, Mamie is not accompanying me to Raleigh.

Mamie and I enjoyed our visit to Chapel Hill. I hope to see you in Raleigh. In any event, please don't hesitate to let me know should you find at any time that you are coming this way.

Sincerely,

By early 1947 Eisenhower had decided to step down as chief of staff, a job he had found even more trying than the occupation. As he wrote to his son, it was "a sorry place to land after having commanded a theatre of war." As chief of staff, he had found himself not only embroiled in the bitter fights over unification and the draft but caught as well between the shrinkage of military resources that was produced by postwar demobilization and the growing demands that were being placed on the military by the expansive new diplomacy of the Cold War. "The World situation presents nothing that can be classed as improvement," he wrote. "Coupled with this is the Congressional determination to slash into budgets that are already practically incapable of carrying out our great bag of commitments, and you can see that our days are anything but hilarious."

In May 1947 he was approached by Thomas J. Watson, the president of IBM and a trustee of Columbia University, who offered him the presidency of the university. Eisenhower had talked before of heading a college or university, and though he doubtless would have preferred a smaller or at least a non-metropolitan institution, he nevertheless accepted Watson's offer. Although he would continue as chief of staff until early 1948, his appointment as president of Columbia was announced in late June 1947.

---

19 July 1947

Dear Swede:

As always your letter provided me with an interesting and sane interlude in an otherwise hectic day. I am truly sorry that you have had to enter the hospital, but I think you are wise in getting a thorough check-up when you find yourself ailing.

There are dozens of different considerations that finally influenced me to say "yes" to the Columbia Trustees. One of these considerations was their clear understanding of the point that I would never really separate myself from the uniformed services of the country. I explained to them carefully that I have lived 36 years in one idea and for one purpose and that as a result I had absorbed several simple conceptions and observations that would remain with me until the end of my days. From my viewpoint, going to Columbia is merely to change the location of my headquarters; perhaps it would be more accurate to say that I am changing the method by which I will continue to strive for the same goals.

I believe fanatically in the American form of democracy—a system that recognizes and protects the rights of the individual and that ascribes to the individual a dignity accruing to him because of his creation in the image of a supreme being and which rests upon the conviction that only through a system of free enterprise can this type of democracy be preserved. Beyond this I believe that world order can be established only by the practice of true cooperation among the sovereign nations and that American leadership toward this goal depends upon her strength—her strength of will, her moral, social and economic strength and, until an effective world order is achieved, upon her military strength. It is these simple conceptions that I will take to Columbia. If by living them and preaching them I can do some good I will hope to stay on indefinitely.

I did not mean suddenly to become pontifical—I have merely been struggling to get over to you something of my basic reasons for deciding to undertake that job when the time comes that The President feels I may be released here. That time, incidentally, is still some months distant.

Additionally, of course, there are certain other influences that affected me. Among these was pressure from a number of different directions to agree to undertake this or that job when this one should be finished for me. Regardless of my regular response that I did not care to think of such things until my period of active service was over, a number of individuals—with their own conceptions concerning the direction in which my duty lay—continued their approaches, sometimes directly, sometimes through close friends. All of them finally understood that I would not consider anything commercial in character; the offers I have received of this type at times appeared to me fantastic. At the very least I have stopped all this by announcing what I hope to do with my personal future.

On the other side of the picture, Mamie and I both hate New York City and recoil from the thought of living there permanently. I know nothing about the workings of a great University and am certainly far from being an "educator." With regard to a residence, I am already searching for a country place somewhere up in the Connecticut area and we confidently expect to live in such a place throughout the year, except possibly for the deep winter months. With regard to the lack of scholarly attainment, the Board of Trustees insists that they want an organizer and a leader, not a professor.

That tells the story in rough, halting fashion. It has been encouraging to receive from many College Presidents and a great number of Professors messages expressing their satisfaction that I have accepted the job.

With regard to John: I think that like all young officers he has of course contemplated the possibility of resigning to enter some civil pursuit. However, I believe it was merely a manifestation of the doubts that nearly always assail a man after he has committed himself to a lifetime of service in one channel—his whole purpose seems to be to improve himself as an Army officer and I think he will stick to it without question.

I have none of the details of my Raleigh trip. Ordinarily I would fly down there in the afternoon, attend the evening meeting and fly back the next morning. If I can possibly see you and Ibby it will provide a real enjoyment to the trip, but from long and bitter experience I have found that my hosts on such occasions usually schedule every possible minute so tightly that there is little time left to do anything else. However, I will have an aide get all the details as soon as possible and I will communicate them to you when I can.

At least, here's hoping.

My very best to both of you and to the children.

As ever,

41

What a letter!—But if you could know how pressed I am you'd understand. [This is a handwritten postscript.]

Eisenhower wrote a brief note to Swede on August 20, inviting Swede to join him in Raleigh where he would be speaking at North Carolina State and dining with the governor. In his reply, on August 20, Swede noted that several newspaper columnists had recently speculated about Eisenhower's political ambitions and declared that "I'd like to back you in a corner in Raleigh to find out if you've changed your mind."

---

25 August 1947

Dear Swede:

Your note just reached me. I am delighted that we shall meet for a few moments in Raleigh, even though I shall apparently have the sketchiest of opportunities to talk to you.

Possibly you can go along with me to my train which I understand is not to pull out until 9:45 and this might give us an opportunity to talk a bit longer. I am due to go to Abilene about October 25 where I will attend a testimonial dinner to Mr. Harger. I would also like to tell you about my latest visit there which took place in June.

Please don't concern yourself about the possibility that I have "changed my mind." You may be certain that I have been absolutely truthful in every public statement I have made on the personal political question and you can be equally sure that I have not directly or indirectly given to anyone the right to represent my feelings and convictions differently at any place or at any time.

It is difficult for many people—particularly those who have led a political life or are engaged in newspaper or radio work—to believe anyone who disclaims political ambition. Even though they may accept without the faintest hint of challenge any statement a man might make about any other subject in the world, on this one thing they maintain a position of doubt, not to say suspicion. Frankly, if Mamie and I could have our way we would, without the slightest hesitation, retire to the quietest and least publicized neighborhood in the United States. We have become convinced that a completely private life is denied us—this conviction, as much as anything else, is at the bottom of my agreement to attempt the job in New York. Beyond this, however, I have no plans, no personal ambitions, and I am attempting to live this as honestly as I say it.

My own deepest concern involves America's situation in the world today. Her security position and her international leadership I regard as matters of the gravest concern to all of us and to our national future. Allied to these questions of course is that of internal health, particularly maximum productivity. While there may be little that I can do about such matters, I do have the satisfaction of feeling that whatever I try to do is on a national and not on any partisan basis. Moreover, I flatter myself to believe that the people who listen to me understand that I am talking or working for all, not for any political party or for any political ambition. This is the attitude I hope that I can preserve to the end of my days.

My very best to Ibby and the girls and, as always, my very best to you.

Sincerely,

Pressure on Eisenhower to become a candidate continued to mount, as did speculation in the press. The latter, Swede wrote on October 25, "has been throwing out so much smoke that, being gullible, I began to suspect at least a spark." If Eisenhower were really determined not to run, Swede asked, shouldn't he "make an unequivocal statement on the subject—one that no one can shoot holes in?"

Dear Swede:

While I have not been invited to the meeting of the North Carolina Press Association in January, it will be impossible for me to attend even if I am asked. My life is just as hectic as ever and I have flatly refused, for many weeks past, to add a single engagement to my schedule. In fact, I have had to break three or four of long standing. At the end of this week I must make a run to Texas and stop at Little Rock on the way back. I am desperately trying to make those my only public appearances during the month except for a two-minute appearance here in the city in an effort to help out the Community Chest campaign.

All the so-called experts in the field of political analysis continuously point out that without artificial stimulus all these "boomlets" for particular individuals sooner or later collapse. I have been pinning my faith and my hopes on the correctness of this assertion—I have made my position very clear and still feel sure that I am not going to be faced with an impossible situation. It has been a most burdensome, not to say annoying, development. It has even resulted in bringing down on my naked head a lot of attacks from people who would ordinarily have no reason for concerning themselves about me one way or the other. But because they see in me some possible thwarting of their own purposes, they use the method of cursing anyone that gets in their way.

Personally I feel that there are a number of candidates in the field who would make acceptable political leaders and I cannot conceive of any set of probable circumstances that would ever convince me that it was my duty to enter such a hectic arena.

I am counting on going to the Army-Navy game this year, primarily because Lord [Harold] Alexander, Governor General of Canada [who had served under Eisenhower in North Africa and Italy], is going to attend and I am rather in the position of being one of his hosts. Frankly, I think I would far rather have the day just to sleep, and read about the results the following morning in the papers. In any event I shall not attend any of the other games.

In Abilene I found that my circle of old acquaintances and friends seems gradually to contract. On this trip I did see Lois Barger Parker—the first time I have seen her since we graduated from high school in 1909. I saw no significant physical change in the town—that is one corner of the country that seems to drift along in the even tenor of its ways, and its people are the happier for it.

It is nice to know that you and your family had such a fine time at the beach. When a whole family loves the sea, the sunlight and deep-sea fishing, it certainly simplifies the vacation problem. With us the matter is somewhat more difficult because Mamie has no interest in outdoor life. I am perfectly ready (always assuming we can get any kind of an opportunity) to go to a mountain stream or a farm with some birds on it or to the seashore. But since none of these places has a definite attraction for Mamie, we always have a big discussion and end up by traveling around and tiring ourselves out. In any event, we are going to take 60 days between the termination of this job and the beginning of the next and incidentally, during that time, I am going to be careful to retain my active duty status.

Give my love to Ibby and the girls, and with warmest regards to yourself,

As ever,

1948

On 22 January 1948, Eisenhower at last put an end to speculation when he released a letter to New Hampshire publisher Leonard V. Finder, in which he wrote that his "decision to remove myself completely from the political scene is definite and positive."

26 January 1948

Dear Swede:

By this time you have possibly noted in the public press that all your remaining questions about a political career for me have been definitely answered. Several of my warm friends—men whose judgment I completely respect—differed from me sharply as to the wisdom of issuing such a statement. In fact, I had only two real supporters, among all my friends, in my belief that I must do so. There were many factors other than those mentioned in my letter to Mr. Finder that had some influence with me but I think I am honest in saying, as I did in the letter, that personal desire and convenience were not predominating among them. Now that it is done, I can at least devote my mind unreservedly to a number of other important things and will not feel like I am constantly on the "witness stand."

I read the letter from your friend [Harold W.] Whicker and I must say that I found it most interesting and intriguing. Discounting or even eliminating his over-generous opinions concerning my personal characteristics and qualifications, the letter is indicative of the thinking of a very, very large number of people in this country today. Most of them, however, have not Mr. Whicker's ability to express himself. Incidentally, some of his sentences are a little on the lengthy side for my simple mind but even so he succeeds in expressing himself clearly and forcefully.

I also read his letter on our educational institutions. You have asked me to return it and I shall do so in a few days but first I think I should like to have a copy of it made because I shall want to refer to it from time to time. My most persistent reaction to his two documents is that it is a tremendous loss to our country that he is a confirmed invalid. We need crusaders; he is obviously the type of man that would never give up in his pursuit of an objective and even though some would certainly accuse him of lopsidedness (I am speaking now particularly of his castigation of our educational system) he would certainly make a lot of complacent, ritualistic people most uncomfortable. If ever I get out in that region I am going to look him up because I have the feeling that an hour's conversation with him would be truly stimulating. When you write to him please assure him of the profound impression his effort made upon me and tell him that the highest praise I can give is: "Our country needs more of his type."

Washington is undergoing a touch of real winter. The temperature must be somewhere around 15 or 20 today and we have quite a bit of snow. The forecaster says we shall continue to have no change for two or three days. I suppose that you have gotten a touch of the same thing down at Chapel Hill.

I have seen pictures of Dick Scott of the Navy [an All-American football player and class president who would soon marry Swede's older daughter] and from them I should say he is a fine-looking boy. I should like to get a chance to have a real talk with him because I should like to subject to microscopic examination every young man fortunate enough to run around with the Hazlett girls.

I do not remember whether I have told you that Mamie and I are counting on being grandparents in early April. Far beyond this, we are already counting on the selection of the school the young grandson or granddaughter (I wish we could figure on twins) is going to attend.

Within ten days or two weeks I expect to turn over this job but I shall be around the city until May 1st, when I go to New York. Right this minute we have a household upset with sickness—Mamie's Dad became quite ill while visiting us. However, anytime you have a chance to get up this way send us a wire and count on staying with us, certainly up to the middle of April—after that we'll always have an extra room in New York.

With love to Ibby and the girls,

As ever,

P.S. Tell Whicker to get a description of the effort being made at Amherst [College] to revitalize educational processes.

On 12 April 1948 Eisenhower wrote Swede a short note, apologizing for its brevity and assuring Swede that "no one writes me letters that are more acceptable and intriguing than yours." He was far more reserved, however, in responding to a proposal that Swede passed along on April 21. An editor at Dodd, Mead and Company, which had published a children's book on submarines by Swede, had proposed that he and Eisenhower "collaborate" on a book based on Eisenhower's Abilene boyhood. While Swede assured Eisenhower that he had "never had even the slightest desire to capitalize in anyway on what is to me a precious friendship," he nevertheless seemed to be genuinely interested in the project. Eisenhower responded with characteristic circumspection, offering to provide Swede with information but carefully maintaining his own distance from the project. Eisenhower's own memoirs, *Crusade in Europe*, was scheduled for publication in the late fall.

28 April 1948

Dear Swede:

In the note I sent just before going on vacation I included my apologies for its brevity. I now repeat them.

I, of course, have no objection whatsoever to your writing any book, article, or pamphlet that you may think worthwhile doing. If the subject should happen to be anything connected with me or my life I would be delighted to provide you with whatever factual information my memory might still retain. On the other hand, I could not be a collaborator in the book—it would have to be your effort alone. As I see it, the difference between you and someone else writing on such a subject is that you are fully acquainted with the Kansas background from which we both came. Moreover, because you are one of my oldest and dearest friends I would spare no pains to help you dig up facts. Beyond this I could not go, and I believe that your publishers are a little bit off the beam in suggesting that we should "collaborate."

If you should decide to undertake such a task you can provide me with a questionnaire and I will do my best to fill it in. The matter, therefore, is strictly between you and your publishers and you can act in the certainty that I will be as helpful as is possible. I should think that the decision you would have to make was whether or not the effort would be worth-while as I cannot conceive that there would be any great demand because here and there in books, articles, and just plain commentary there has been an awful lot written about the Eisenhower tribe. It is only fair to say, however, that while it all has pretended to be factual reporting some of it has gone deeper into the fictional world than you would possibly dream of doing even in a book that was frankly fictional.

I did not do any fishing on my vacation. Mamie and I simply went down to Augusta National with a few friends and lived on the golf course there for 10 days. Incidentally, I did not improve my playing a bit, but I did have a whale of a lot of fun. It was the best two weeks I have had in many years.

I cannot be sure what my schedule calls for on the 6th of June [when Swede's daughter was scheduled to marry Richard Scott]. It is my impression that that is the exact date of one of the busy commencement programs at Columbia. However, I assure you that even if I could get off for a few hours in the afternoon and fly to your daughter's wedding, to return that evening to New York, I would feel it a great privilege to do so. Won't you please write to me again at Columbia University about the end of May to remind me to make a special effort?

One of the reasons I accepted the Columbia job was because I thought that while doing something useful I would still be in a position to relax a bit; to base myself better than I have been able to do for the past many years. My schedule of appointments for the first month there has already grown to appalling proportions. If current indications provide any index of what my future life there is to be, I shall quit them cold, and deliberately go to some foresaken spot on the earth's surface to stay until I am fully ready to go back to work on the only basis that it appears I am ever to be allowed to work, namely under full [and] heavy steam.

I do not know whether you occasionally make trips to New York to see your publishers. If you do, you can always count with certainty upon a warm welcome at our house and a roof under which to lay your head. You know that there could be no more welcome guests for us than you and Ibby.

Last weekend I went to Kansas. I tried desperately to avoid making the trip because it cropped off the last three days of my planned vacation. However, Mr. Harger, who is about the only man of the older generation left that helped me get into West Point, made the invitation so personal that I felt I had to go. The meeting was at Wichita but a few Abilene-ites headed by Mr. Harger were present for the luncheon. I was in the city only a matter of two or three hours.

With love to the family and warmest regard to yourself,

As ever,

Eisenhower was to be formally installed as president of Columbia University on 12 October 1948 and had invited Swede and his wife to attend. In his letter of September 28, Swede had expressed relief at Eisenhower's decision to steer clear of politics but had also observed that only that morning a columnist had "intimated that you and George [E.] Allen were conniving on the Democratic nomination in 1952!" Allen was a lawyer and businessman with an ingratiating sense of humor and a flair for cultivating the friendship of Washington's politically powerful, including Franklin Roosevelt, Harry Truman (who in 1945 appointed Allen director of the Reconstruction Finance Corporation), and Dwight Eisenhower. He later wrote about his experiences in a book entitled *Presidents Who Have Known Me* (1960 ed., New York: Simon & Schuster).

---

6 October 1948

Dear Swede:

I am not astonished that you find it impossible to come to the party here on the 12th. It will be quite a formalized affair and the crowd will make impossible any real contact with such old friends as may come. From my viewpoint, I would far rather you make a trip to New York at a less hectic period—in which case we could really make some progress in settling the world's major problems. Incidentally, I think I have told you there is always room for you and Ibby in our house whenever you can come this way.

I tender my most sincere sympathy in the loss of your dog. You do not have to describe to me what he meant to you, but I do hope you will be successful in finding his brother to take his place.

While many people have tried to make something of my friendship with George Allen, the fact is that it is just that and nothing more. His wife and mine have been very close friends for years, and I met George at the beginning of the war. Since that time my contacts with him have brought me nothing but satisfaction; he has never attempted to dump any kind of problem, political or otherwise, in my lap. He is one of those delightful persons who has a rollicking attitude toward life and he himself is always the butt of his innumerable stories and jokes. In addition to all this, he has behind his clownish exterior a very shrewd clear-thinking brain. If ever you meet him you will understand what I mean.

You mention some columnist saying that George and I were conniving for the 1952 nomination. He unquestionably got his lead on that one from a telecast made by George Allen during the Democratic Convention. Some reporter asked him a question, "Are you for Eisenhower for President?" Quick as a flash he replied, "Of course, like everybody else I think he would make the best President this country ever had, but I am for him in 1952 not 1948." That is the sole incident when I have heard George say anything about 1952, and he was definitely kidding a reporter.

I had no idea that I was putting you on the spot in my answer to your query about a story on our youthful days in Abilene. To correct that error, I simply give you carte blanche to quote me as you please on that subject—if you want to tell your publisher that I violently object, go right ahead. On the other hand, if someone is going to write that kind of a story I secretly would rather have you do it than anyone else. I still fail to see, however, how any great amount of interest could be engendered in a story of the commonplace happenings involving a bunch of boys in a small western town of forty-five years ago.

My love to the family and, as always, warmest regards to yourself,

Sincerely,

1949

The National Security Act of 1947, which had effected a partial unification of the armed services, did little to diminish interservice rivalry. Indeed, the battles of the late 1940s were among the bitterest in service history. At stake was which branch would take the lead in implementing the nation's emerging nuclear weapons strategy. The navy's hope rested with a new class of "super carriers" which would be capable of handling B-29 bombers carrying atomic bombs. The air force, on the other hand, countered with the new long-range B-36 bomber. Secretary of Defense Louis Johnson's April 1949 decision to halt construction of the "super carrier" USS *United States* prompted the resignation of Secretary of the Navy John L. Sullivan and led to an angry attack on the administration by high-ranking naval officers.

---

27 April 1949

Dear Swede:

Your splendid letter reached me while I was in Key West and I still was very miserable from a queer sort of digestive or stomach disorder. In the last two or three weeks I have improved markedly. For the past two weeks Mamie has been with me here at the Augusta National Golf Club and I have been puttering around with a bit of golf every day. I expect to be down here for another week as a minimum.

I have not your letter with me for the moment and, consequently, cannot discuss intelligently the various and interesting points you raised—however, I do recall your expression of fear that I should not appreciate the true value of the carrier. I am quite certain that no one has a greater respect for the carrier task force, under conditions suited to its use, than I do. Moreover, I believe it is one of the finest weapons that we can maintain in our Arsenal of Defense because of the great flexibility permitted in its use during the early days of an emergency when we know that everything is going to be different from what we had previously anticipated. I would be among the last people in the world to consent, in these days and times, to the elimination of the carrier from the U.S. Navy. I believe that most people hold similar views although there seems to be vast differences of opinion concerning the types and numbers of carriers that we should attempt to maintain in time of peace. There is, as you know, a tremendous argument going on about the wisdom of building the so-called Super-Carrier. I certainly do not pretend to know the answer to this one.

The great difficulty comes about through the tendency of each Service to measure its importance to the country in terms of the size of its current budget. The struggle for the lion's share of the defense dollar is never ended—it is conducted relentlessly and endlessly, in the Halls of Congress, in the public press and in inter-Service argument and conferences. All of these arguments carry great air of authenticity because of the fact that a democracy will always have an obvious deficit in the desirable strength of its security establishment. But since a democracy must always retain a waiting, strategically defensive, attitude it is mandatory that some middle line be determined between desirable strength and unbearable cost. Since, therefore, each Service always will have less strength than it considers necessary, it can always develop plausible, and sometimes bitter, argument for greater and greater appropriations. What we must do is to forget and abandon this type of approach. We must put our consolidated professional brains to the job of determining the general character of the defense establishment when needed and these same professionals should logically reach conclusions as to proper priorities in producing such defensive strength under limited budgets. Stated in a crude and incomplete way, this is the problem of today.

Frankly, I have found many of our younger officers showing greater appreciation of these facts than I have discovered among our seniors. I do not despair of the future because I believe the younger generation has more sense than ours has so far displayed. But I must say that the current task of getting every one to approach these questions from the single viewpoint of the country's good—and without unreasonable prejudice or bias in favor of some particular theory or weapon is truly difficult. For this situation I blame no one, nor any particular service—at least I attach to no one else any more fault than I do to myself, but I am quite certain that unless we rapidly arrive at some sensible solution of this problem we are going to damage the country financially and without adding to its defensive strength.

The subject is no longer discussed, in Washington, in terms other than those of controversy. If someone expresses doubt as to the great effectiveness of the B-36, then he is instantly "anti-Air"; if someone else sees weakness in the theory of employing a super-carrier or mildly objects to the Navy's developing a land Army, in time of war, of 600,000 Marines (which it did in World War II), then he is called "anti-Navy."

All this distresses me greatly. I have been very proud of membership in the Armed Services and have felt that, jointly, they provided to the country the greatest body of honest, selfless, intelligent public servants that could be found anywhere. Consequently, it hurts me to see a public impression growing up that these men do nothing except to quarrel and fight among themselves for access to the taxpayers' pocketbook. Most of the time and in most problems they work together beautifully and are in complete accord. Such things do not, however, make "news"; seemingly, only the quarrel can do this. Consequently, our Armed Services and their military leaders are getting a bad name, most of which is undeserved, but for which there is, unfortunately, some foundation.

I did not mean to grow so garrulous this morning.

Give my love to Ibby and the children, and of course, warm regards to yourself. In all this Mamie joins me enthusiastically.

As ever,

The National Security Act Amendments of 1949 increased the authority of the secretary of defense and further reduced the autonomy of the individual services. The angry debate over the naval budget and over plans for the supercarrier continued unabated, however. Swede, of course, took the navy's side, referring to Louis Johnson, the new secretary of defense, as a "bozo" with an "anti-Navy bias."

---

12 August 1949

Dear Swede:

Since you have called my attention to the point, I now realize that I do answer your letters far more promptly than I do those that reach me from most other people. The reason—from my viewpoint—is a simple one. Yours are interesting, and the others usually fall into one of three categories. The first category comprises requests of various kinds for help. Sometimes this is merely money begging, more often it is a request that I use some fancy "influence" for everything from obtaining scarce theater tickets to obtaining civil service positions in our occupation forces.

The second category is made up of advice, usually from strangers, and its purpose is to tell me what my duty is and what I am to do about it. Like the first category, the subject matter of this covers a very wide range.

The third category involves invitations to dinners, to conventions, to university ceremonies, to luncheons, dinners, breakfasts—it would be impossible to indicate the scope if I would fill up this page with words. Only a few others—indeed a very very few—write to me as you do, merely as a friend who seems to get some kick out of receiving my answers.

Of course I was tremendously intrigued to have your reaction on "unification." Right now I am a member of a Board which has been meeting here in Denver for the last two days. It was appointed by the Secretary of Defense (Forrestal) [James V. Forrestal, who resigned in early 1949 and committed suicide a few months later] to examine the entire subject of Academy education in the three Services with particular emphasis on the possibility of using these years of education to promote ultimate unification.

I don't know when I have undertaken anything (even though I went on this Board with extreme reluctance) that has given me so much encouragement in the pursuit of real and sensible progress. In the first place, the Board is made up of a very fine group of educators. Associated with it are a number of Panels each of which, in turn, comprises a group of outstanding men. All of these people have given earnest and effective attention to the problems at hand.

You will be interested to know that the education records of West Point and Annapolis have received the highest praise from this entire group, although it is clear that some of these people entered upon their examination with preconceived ideas that they would find nothing except the things to criticize. Comparative records established in many colleges through examination upon graduation show that the Academies stand exceedingly high. About the only real criticism voiced by this group of educators was that little was to be found in the curricula and methods at West Point and Annapolis that encouraged free-thinking and self-confidence.

Far more encouraging to me however, than these pleasing reports upon two institutions that so deeply involve our sentiments, was the obvious interest taken by all my associates in analyzing the need for teamwork among the Services and in their development of ideas as to how this could be secured. Every conceivable kind of idea was discussed and a wide variety of viewpoints was brought to bear. However, the whole thing was done in an atmosphere of friendliness and I am quite sure that every participant believed that much has been accomplished. This Board and its Panels have been meeting intermittently for some months and I am certain that out of its work is going to come much that is good. Incidentally, I met for the first time, Admiral [Raymond A.] Spruance. Frankly I think he is one of the finest Naval officers I have ever met. He is quiet, modest, and self-confident without being either dominus or patronizing. I like him extremely and wish I could have had more time with him.

Incidentally, and before I drop completely the subject of this recent Board, the studies reveal that the curriculum at West Point is somewhat more crowded and intensive and requires a greater number of hours of work than at Annapolis. Some years ago I think the reverse was true, and I thank the Lord that I went through the Academy when they were not so much engaged in the cramming business. Frankly I honestly believe it far easier if we do not place too much dependence in mere knowledge—in other words, I do not believe too much in cramming.

With respect to the carrier, I do not follow your argument about the so called "super ship." If an Air Force bomber cannot penetrate into the heart-land, then how is this going to be done by a bomber flying off a super carrier? Each will admittedly have to fly far beyond the range limit of fighter planes. Consequently, while I hold to my opinion that a certain number of so called "freak" ["fleet"] carriers can be a most favorable element in our defensive structure, I do not see how we can give the super carrier a sufficiently high place in our priorities that we can afford to build them in an era when we are going to face smaller and smaller appropriations. Please do not for one moment interpret my words to mean that I would not like to see a vast amount of this practical experimentation—provided the Nation could afford it. Finally, there must however be a line drawn between the requirements of economy on one side, and hope for improvement in our defense establishment on the other.

In this whole discussion about unification there has developed a lot of froth and fuming, and a lot of heat, much of which was completely unjustified. No one has really plugged for a lop-sided single arm of defense organization. No one has advocated any "all the eggs in one basket" type of philosophy. These expressions and ideas are first used, in my opinion, by someone who argues hotly for a particular detail and soon there develops an attempt to smear each side of the argument, by the other, by all types of extravagant expressions and which, while he may develop some public or even Congressional support, are usually proof of nothing more than the mental poverty of their originators. In all this no one party has been soley guilty, just as no one has been completely innocent. It seems to me that lately there has been a very great decrease in this type of thing and I honestly believe that notable progress already made in unification is not only indicative of a greater application of good sense and less temper, but implies also a still greater progress for the future.

Louis Johnson may make mistakes, but I believe he is thoroughly and completely determined to turn in the finest possible performance that he can. You say he has an "anti-Navy" slant, but I doubt such a generalization is completely accurate. I know that he came into his present job with the feeling that our present Navy could scarcely be justified on the basis of the naval strength of any potential enemy particularly when it is clear that any other navy worthy of the name belongs to a traditional ally. On the other hand he, like everybody else, had and has a healthy respect for hostile submarines and he was very anxious that the Navy consolidate all resources and brains in the field of anti-submarine warfare. I have never found Secretary Johnson opposing anything for the Navy that appeared clearly needful in the combating of the submarine for the complete control of the seas. I know that in some instances he has approved measures and forces that he considered over-generous for these purposes. He, like most others, clearly recognizes that the greatest point of argument between the Navy and Air Force is the extent to which we should plan a Navy to take part in bombing operations against inland targets and where the effect upon the control of the seas is necessarily, more or less, indirect.

There are of course dozens of lesser problems and a myriad of details on which arguments develop, but fundamentally all of them finally come back to the one basic question.

One of the lesser problems you have already mentioned—the mission, strength and armament of the Marines. For example, all airplanes fly off a land base or a floating base; why then must we have a third Air Force when we already have one each for the floating and the land bases? Until World War I the Marines were never used in a formation as large as a brigade. The question naturally arises; why has it become suddenly necessary to develop a Marine force of hundreds of thousands in war and carry, in time of peace, the great financial burden of preparing for such a war time force?

Another item; for many years, starting first in 1930, I have been one of those in the Army who insisted on getting rid of ocean-going Transport Services. During all the years that I was a junior officer I was slapped down on this argument by my superiors. Finally I became Chief of Staff and I asked Admiral Nimitz whether he would take over the whole organization since I was now in a position to do something. I was astonished to find that the Navy did not want it because they thought that the Army was trying to make a "service organization" out of the Navy. At the same time I was opposed by most of my own people, particularly by those holding high positions in our "Transport Service," but the real block at that time was the Navy didn't want it. Now I note that since Louis Johnson has gone into office that this move has been made. I cannot say who is completely right because only experience will show whether we have greater efficiency with less costs and whether the needs of all Services in any possible emergency will be better fulfilled, but the point is that at last someone is in a position to make a decision and to make it stick.

Possibly in my enthusiasm in the young officer I may have over-stated my case. I do not mean to say that a young officer twenty years from now will be as much of a fuddy-duddy as I am, or as some of those who twenty years ago appeared to me to be blocking all progress. What I was really trying to emphasize was that the Army and Navy, by their nature, can fall into the administrative hands of oldsters. Maybe I could express my thought a little better by saying that for every General or flag officer over fifty-five I should really like to see one not over thirty-five. Of course I realize that such a statement is on the cock-eyed side. The applicable actuarial data would finally defeat this unless every once in awhile you should find one of these high ranking officers when he was about forty years old. Unfortunately the calendar will not stand still when we find a brilliant fellow when he is thirty or forty.

You mentioned in your letter that one of your friends kidded you about me being *back* in politics—for me you can say that I consider him some kind of a "blankety-blank-blank," for if he can show for once that I have been in politics, he has no right to use the word politics. Moreover, you are most assuredly right that nothing has happened that has changed the convictions I expressed a couple of years ago. You may be quite sure that if anything ever occurs that appears so cataclysmic as to cause me to change in this regard you will be one of the first to know it. So in the absence of such unforeseen and catastrophical development you just go right ahead on the line you are pursuing.

It was nice to have the news of your daughter and her new husband. I have heard much about Spike Fahrion. All of it good. Incidentally, it is astonishing how many of your old friends and shipmates I have run into. Most of them seem to know that you

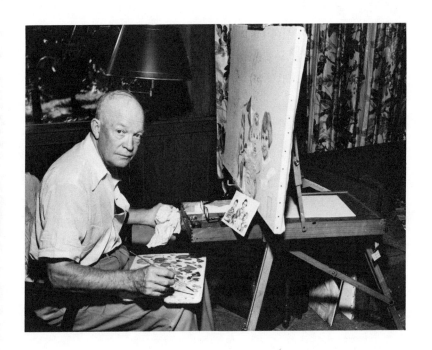

Eisenhower at Camp David, Maryland, 1 August 1954 (United States Navy photograph, courtesy of Dwight D. Eisenhower Library).

and I have been life-long friends and I have been most pleased by the fact that I can give them news of you.

One last word, because of your question about my painting, it is rank hypocrisy to allow what I do to go under such an exalted name, as I am a deliberate dauber. It is easy enough to do if you are fortunate enough to have a place to permit your easel, paint and wet canvas to stand. It becomes a little difficult when you must clear them away after each ten minute tour at the canvas. Personally, I was almost fired because of my deficiency at drawing at West Point and I have nothing whatsoever of artistic talents. I simply get a bang out of working with colors and occasionally one of my efforts comes out with sufficient appeal about it to entice some of my friends to steal it and carry it away. Many others find their way to the waste paper basket. If you are interested I would be pleased to tell you how I got started, the materials I use and so on. Most of mine are done between eleven and twelve-thirty at night, but I can guarantee you that if you ever take it up it will consume so many of your vertical hours that you will wonder how they have ever slipped away from you.

Mamie and I send love to you and your nice family. We are still looking forward to the day you can visit us in New York.

Cordially,

Further reductions in the navy's budget, together with the cancellation of the supercarrier, eventually led to the so-called revolt of the admirals, to an acrimonious congressional hearing, and to the dismissal of Adm. Louis E. Denfeld, the chief of naval operations.

---

17 November 1949

Dear Swede:

Your letter of the 2nd seemed to me to be so full of misinterpretations of what I thought I had said to you in the past that I was bewildered—until I had the idea of sending for a copy of the letter I wrote to you from Denver. Never again am I going to write a letter that must be dispatched under the "dictated but not read" category. To illustrate how badly garbled that letter was I use only one example: In one place where I said "fleet carriers" I found the worthy sergeant transformed it into "freak carriers."

Consequently, rather than review the entire file of correspondence, I think that I shall merely, on the basis of your latest communication, set down a few of my opinions or convictions and hereafter use this effort as the "alpha" of my running essay effort, of which, of course, you will be the entire reading public.

To deal first with the most important point of all, I very much doubt that Mamie and I shall get to the Army-Navy game. We have just returned from a four day visit to Annapolis and that represents about all the time we have to spare before we take off for Texas on the last day of the month for a two weeks' stay. However, it is remotely possible that, even at the very last instant, we may find it possible to go.

Because there are a number of subjects, not all of them related, which I would like to mention in this letter, I am going to do so rather briefly. I hope that this will not mean to you that I am arbitrary about any of them. There are few—maybe none—concerning which I would not quickly change my opinion if someone should present to me an argument that struck me as applicable and convincing.

First—I have long advocated the peacetime maintenance and operation of a number of so-called "fleet carriers." The convincing reason for doing so is, to my mind, the flexibility of this particular weapon. It should be useful in almost any corner of the globe and since every war starts under unforeseen circumstances, it strikes me as good insurance to have something that could be used, under current conditions of warfare, anytime and, with obvious limitations with respect to land masses, anywhere.

Having said this much, the question becomes, in a limited budget, how many of these can we afford to keep in action during years of peace? This is admittedly a very difficult question, and the Navy opinion should be more influential than that of any other professional service. Nevertheless, all Services are forced into the problem because the matter finally becomes one of dipping ten glasses of water out of a six-glass bucket. We must never lose sight of the fact than an over-riding priority for a reasonable number of combat units does not necessarily mean an indefinite or additional number of these same units should take priority over all other classes of weapons and engines of war.

It was on questions such as this that the recent "war" broke out in Washington, and I tell you frankly that I was discouraged and saddened by the whole business. Because of the pressure of time I cannot expand too greatly upon this subject. But I cannot help but feel some resentment toward those who started this open warfare, with its resultant loss of confidence among great sections of our people in the judgment, selflessness, and integrity of their military leaders.

With respect to the super-carrier I think that in some one of my letters I must have expressed my views on this particular subject. I agree with you that, if we are down to the basic question of survival in a force-driven world, and if we are efficiently and effectively using every dollar that the Congress gives for security purposes, then considerations of economy cannot validly be advanced against defense requirements. In attempting to assist Mr. Forrestal (and later Mr. Johnson) I have studied dozens of specific projects for saving money without hurting or diminishing our combat forces. It is possible that every answer I have received has been completely logical and correct. At least they all—(with only occasional minor exceptions)—argue that there is no possibility of saving in overhead, administrative, and routine costs without damaging directly and seriously our combat forces. I could discuss various aspects of this with you by the hour—here I can say only that I believe, with Mr. Johnson, that if we really put our hearts into the job, both by individual Service and by unified effort, that we can save millions. Nevertheless, I doubt that we could save, by these methods, enough money to build a super-carrier and at the same time procure all those other valuable items that probably have, in the minds of most, equal or greater priority than the super-carrier. Strangely enough, after many witnesses in the recent investigation had deprecated and belittled the effects of strategic bombing, they—the same witnesses—urged the need for the super-carrier and development of the long range bombing planes that would fly off its decks. It seems to me that there are obvious internal contradictions in any such argument. Moreover, if anyone ever convinces me that a "super-carrier" is essential to the control of the seas, I'll be for that, too!!

I think that you will find my past letters full of expressions exhibiting concern for "American control of the seas." Nobody will fight harder and longer for a Navy adequate to perform this function than I will. Moreover, I think that I shall probably be as liberal as most in my readiness to agree that numbers of missions become part of the function of controlling the sea that do not confine themselves to the mere attack of Naval targets. I can see that many operations against ports, submarine installations, coastal communication centers and the like, while actually conducted over the land, are designed for direct assistance in controlling the seas. But when the relationship between the specific attack and the control of the seas becomes so tenuous, and the support so indirect, that the Navy assumes responsibility for attacking targets in the very heart of the enemy homeland, then I can say that we have either gone far afield in the allocation of tasks or (and this is always possible) our idea of coordination among the three Services on the basis of mutually supporting missions is a completely false one.

If we adhere to current doctrine and are not ready to meet each other on a basis of mutual confidence and trust, I could understand an argument that might be advanced by the Air Corps about as follows: "Give the Navy everything it needs to control the seas: ships, guns, Marines, airplanes, and let the Navy organize those as it pleases. But give the Air Forces everything they need to bomb the enemy strong points: industrial centers, transportation systems, etc., etc. If this means that one or more of the Air Forces' landing fields should be mobile, and maintained on the sea, then also give the Navy enough services to protect our field. In other words, the "super-carrier" would belong, under this argument, to the Air Forces!

Personally, I am very strong for the Navy, but I venture to doubt its effectiveness in bombing the Victoria Falls. This attitude, on my part, shows an even greater concern for the primary Navy mission, control of the seas, than is exhibited by those who want the Navy to do everything from pole to pole. At least, I think I have demonstrated that in the arguments that develop when all of these serious questions are dragged out before the public and each debater attempts to capture the interest and the vote of the public, there is no limit to the potential distortion, confusion, and emotional heat in which these subjects will be surrounded.

I was somewhat astonished to read your reservations about [Adm. Forrest P.] Sherman. Whenever, in previous letters, you have mentioned him, it has always been in glowing terms. Certainly your good opinion has had considerable influence in the development of my own. For my part I have, as yet, found no reason for any change. When Sherman was representing the Navy in the writing of the unification law two years ago he was an extraordinarily able and tireless advocate of the Navy position. I have never seen any slightest swerving in his belief in the Navy's mission and in naval efficiency, loyalty, and integrity. While no one asked me for recommendations concerning the identify of a new CNO [chief of naval operations], it is quite true that I have frequently expressed quite favorable opinions about Sherman, in the presence both of my superiors and of others. It is always possible that these may have swayed some others, including those in authority. If this should, by chance be true, I assure you that it was your expressed opinions as well as my own beliefs that were responsible for my statements.

Only the other day I had a long talk with Sherman at Annapolis. I took at least ten minutes to express to him your sentiments of respect, admiration, and liking. I also told him of my hope that he would someday have an opportunity to drop by Chapel Hill and talk to you, because I thought any man in the Service today would profit from listening to the results of your study, reflection and experience. If I have erred as seriously as your letter now indicates, I am in a hell of a spot. (However, don't let it worry you. I have been in much worse ones and gotten out of them safely.)

Actually, there were a dozen other subjects I was going to take up in this letter. I now find that everytime I start talking about these matters at all, my anxiety to be completely fair and square leads me into so many divergent directions that it is impossible to discuss them adequately in a letter. Someday we simply must get together for a couple of days of undisturbed conversation.

Give my love to Ibby and the girls.

As ever,

Eisenhower replied to a Christmas card from Swede in a short note dated 21 December 1949, then returned to the exchange over Admiral Sherman the following day.

---

22 December 1949

Dear Swede:

Apparently my most recent letter to you tended to excite you a bit. I hope it did not raise your blood pressure beyond the blow-off point.

I think that now I have a clear picture of your estimate of Sherman. While it is true that this estimate is somewhat different from what I thought it was, some months ago, yet my own acquaintanceship with the man, added to what I thought, originally, was your opinion, gave me a composite reading that was not greatly different from the one you now present. No harm has been done.

Churning around in the back of my mind is the impression that I may have already answered your letter on this point. If I have, just take this repetition as another indication of approaching senility, and throw the thing in the wastebasket. At least, nothing will be hurt if I send you, even for the second time, very best wishes from Mamie and me for a fine Christmas and a 1950 crowded with good things for all the Hazlett family.

Cordially,

1950

By the time he wrote this letter, and despite claims to the contrary, Eisenhower had begun to sound more and more like a candidate. He entertained a steady stream of visitors, including New York's Governor Thomas E. Dewey, the unsuccessful Republican candidate for the presidency in 1948, all of whom urged him to run. And though he continued to disavow political ambitions, both publicly and in private, his speeches and correspondence took on an increasingly conservative and ideological tone as he inveighed against "statism" and called for a return to the "middle way."

24 February 1950

Dear Swede:

Naturally, I cannot challenge your assertion that I had to take the red ink, but I do repudiate your additional postulate that I had to "like" it. To prove my point I am taking advantage of your approaching anniversary (or its approximation, in view of the leap year uniqueness of your birthdate) to send you a new typewriter ribbon. If on arrival, it appears to be packaged in a way that you do not like, I hope that you will find it possible to exchange for one you really want.[1] My additional hope is that, in black print, I shall occasionally get a letter that is as interesting and completely intriguing as your latest one to me.

In its reading, it took me half of the first page to decide that you had not gone a bit balmy. This, because of the fact that I had not previously seen the story about the "best dressed men"; I had not even heard of it. My reaction is that some people must not have a hell of a lot to do if they have time to devote themselves to such drivel. My clothes are made by a Jewish friend of mine who has been in the men's tailoring business all his life. He has one or two tailors who make clothing on the "special order" basis. Since my friend keeps my measurements on hand, he comes up here with a new suit every several months, usually of a cloth and cut of his own choosing. So far as my own intervention in such matters is concerned, one of Mamie's chief causes of complaint is that I will not even buy a pair of socks for myself. She keeps in constant touch with my friend [Sarg. John] Moanny (a Negro who has lived with me since the very first days of the war) in order that she can keep me stocked with the necessaries of decent existence. This constitutes my entire knowledge of my own sartorial requirements and equipment.

Gordon Gray strikes me as being a citizen of fine character and sensibilities.[2] He is endowed with good judgment and a likeable personality. I do not suppose that you would class him as an intellectual giant, but such people are usually uncomfortable characters to have around anyway. I understand that he is a wealthy individual—which won't be any handicap in the running of a modern university. I predict that he will eventually achieve a high place in the affections of the University family in Chapel Hill, including the faculty portion.

Like you, I was somewhat astonished that Milton finally made

1. Swede had typed his letter of February 19 with a red ribbon on his "ancient Corona." The package that Eisenhower refers to was a new Royal typewriter.
2. Gray, whose family held a controlling interest in the R. J. Reynolds Tobacco Company, had held a number of positions in the Truman administration, including that of secretary of the army, and had recently been appointed president of the University of North Carolina.

up his mind to leave Kansas State.[3] He was well situated there and his standing with the Regents and the Legislature was well exemplified when his most recent budget was not only approved in detail but, in certain important particulars, was increased over the amounts he requested. Recently the authorities completely remodeled his house, to include full air conditioning—something that is really more than a convenience in Kansas summers, as you well know. His state-wide standing was comparable and he was in constant demand in all the larger centers as a speaker and a distinguished guest. Moreover, he has been offered the Presidency of several other universities, including one or two quite large ones where pay and perquisites far exceeded what he was getting at Kansas State. Some of these he refused to consider for a single moment because of what he deemed to be unsatisfactory academic standards.

In my opinion, the decisive factors in finally taking him to Pennsylvania State were purely personal. First, he has gotten to the point where the doctors urge upon him some regular outdoor recreation and Kansas offers little or none of this in the only thing he really likes—fresh water fishing. Pennsylvania's streams and lakes are numerous, and most of them provide exactly the kind of outdoor sport that he loves. On top of this is the fact that his wife's parents live in Washington, D.C. One of our brothers lives near Pittsburgh and so, by coming East, both sides of the family tend to find greater family companionship than they do in the West. You must realize that, since our father and mother died, there remains in Kansas among our close relatives only [my brother] Roy's widow and one of her daughters. Of course, the greatly increased pay and emoluments that go with the presidency of Penn State can scarcely be considered as drawbacks.

I have read some of the same comments that you have concerning my alleged dissatisfaction with my present position! They are merely examples of distortion and inaccuracy. It is true that in attempting, at times, to explain to my friends the difficulties

---

3. Milton Eisenhower, Ike's youngest brother, had served in a variety of governmental posts before becoming president of Kansas State University in 1943. In 1950 he assumed the presidency of Pennsylvania State University. In 1956 he became president of Johns Hopkins, a post that he held until his retirement in 1967.

of my present life, I have dwelt upon the conflicts that arise between the details of university administration, unusually persistent adhesions from a past life, and, finally, the demands that arise out of my earnest effort to be of some help to people who are struggling manfully to support the essentials of the American way of life. Actually, I believe that if a man were able to give his full or nearly full attention to such a job as this, he would find it completely absorbing. On a campus like Columbia's, the greatest opportunity is that of meeting constantly with fine minds, in every kind of discipline. Because I love to partake in or, at least, to listen to discussions on such subjects as economics, history, contemporary civilization, some branches of natural and physical science, public health and engineering, you can see that living with a distinguished faculty gives to me many wonderful hours that I could never have in any other environment. Sometimes, however, my loyalties to several different kinds of purposes lead me into a confusing, not to say almost nerve-wearing, kind of living. At such times, just as anyone else would do, I unquestionably express myself in tones of irritation and resentment, and I have no doubt that a chance listener could interpret some of these expressions as irritation with my "apparently" sole preoccupation—that of administering the affairs of this great University. Actually, such outbursts (which, of course, are nothing but a manifestation of a soldier's right to grouse) are directed at myself for allowing confusion and uncertainty to arise where system and serenity should prevail. I hope you can make out what I am getting at but, in any event, I do assure you that, if I were convinced that I had made a mistake in coming to Columbia, I am not so stupid as to fail to recognize the instant and obvious cure. As long as I am here, you can believe that I am not only interested in the task, but I still believe it to offer a way in which I may render some service to the public at large.

With respect to my political difficulties, it is a curious fact that, while little mention of them is made nowadays in the public press, I am by no means free of the problem. A quite steady stream of visitors, to say nothing of correspondence, reaches me under one excuse or another, and with the frequent consequence of long political discussion that rarely fails to drag me, as an individual, into future speculation. I have heard much of my "clear duty" and have learned to answer this by inquiring as to the comparable duty of my caller. It is astonishing how frequently the conversation can instantly be turned, by this query, into other channels. However, the attempt sometimes backfires, particularly when I learn that an individual has devoted time and effort and a great portion of his substance to the attempt to counteract government by bureaucracy and the discernible drift toward statism. Since I abhor these two things, you can see that occasionally I get myself into a conversational morass.

Fortunately, these incidents are not of great frequency, but on the other side of the picture, they usually involve people of prominence, who, therefore, cannot be disregarded. In some instances, I have the utmost respect for their expressed convictions. Some are businessmen, some are avowed politicians, some seem to be only public-spirited citizens and some can be considered no less than statesmen. In any case, I am merely trying to let you see that the problem is not entirely a thing of the past. It often plagues me at present and some people seem to think it has a future. This last, at least, I do not admit.

I do not recall the exact terms in which I previously expressed to you my opinion of Louis Johnson. I am quite sure, however, that those terms have never included the word "profound." I am convinced he is honest but he is, of course, avowedly a *politician and he is impulsive.* These last two factors lead him to believe that the public likes rapid, even spectacular, decisions. Couple this attitude with a conviction that we had better economize or we are going to lose the things that are of the greatest value to us, and I think it is not too difficult to understand his general motivation.

You will recall that, for a number of weeks after Mr. Johnson first took office, he insisted upon my remaining rather regularly in Washington to consult with him and with other responsible officials of the Security Establishment. In recent months, he has not continued this insistence. While I am obviously welcome in his office, he no longer seems to sense the need he once expressed constantly and urgently. This change, I have no doubt, comes about because of increased confidence on his own part as well as a possible feeling that I do not fit into a situation which, after all—from his viewpoint—is political and partisan as well as professional and national. Moreover, he has Bradley as Chairman of the JCS and cannot, by any means, ignore his position and counsel. I know that you do not consider him an ideal public servant in his present post; but will you name any individual—who could be considered reasonably available—that you would think ideal?

I admire and like Spike Fahrion so it is not difficult for me to go along with a great portion of the Service quarrel analysis that he sent to you. I must remark, however, that it is almost impossible for any Service person to achieve a completely objective and disinterested viewpoint toward the development and incidents of that whole unfortunate episode. Actually, I think that you and I could probably come as close to achieving this attitude as could anyone; you, for the reason that you are naturally fair and just by temperament and were removed from the scene both geographically and functionally, while I, because of my wartime post and the way in which I was used, while in Washington, by the Commander in Chief. You, of course, saw nothing but a rather amusing and even slightly ridiculous aspect to the last two sentences of Spike's presentation. [Fahrion had closed his analysis of the "revolt of the admirals" by remarking that "someone facetiously said last night that the solution to the whole problem was to have the Army join the Marines, and the Air Force the Naval Air; then make Johnson SecNav and the whole problem of unification would be solved. Not so farfetched at that, when you consider we have been running a unified show for many years."] Yet to such people as Bradley and [Air Force Chief of Staff Gen. Hoyt S.] Vandenberg, those two sentences, which for many months have been bandied about Washington's cocktail lounges, presented something more than mere cause for a chuckle. They were acutely aware of the fact that the proposition was more than once suggested with some seriousness, at one time, apparently, with deadly earnestness. So far as I am concerned, I have always felt that if we could see anything logical in turning the whole job over to one Service I would be very glad to have the others bow out of the whole picture, no matter which ones might be involved.

But I have earnestly supported the proposition that each Service has an indispensable role in the provision of reasonable national security and that, if it will only perform that role adequately, it will have little time to devote to invasion of the missions of others. I think the sad part of the whole business is that each Service is seemingly incapable of confining itself to its own obvious tasks, but rather feels a compulsion—in order that it may demonstrate its own importance and indispensability—to assert a competency in the performance of other Security tasks which it does not and should not possess.

You may have read my testimony before the Investigating Committee or, if not, you may have seen the recent article, in *U.S. News and World Report*, in which I expressed my views on these points. Certainly I believe that there is in each Service the brains to do the job right if only each can become *respectful of the importance of its own task* and does not feel it necessary to try to grab off the jobs of others.

So far as Mr. Johnson's economy measures are concerned, there is a very long story involved. I do know that he has asserted a hope of saving money without hurting combat strength—and after many, many years in Washington, both in subordinate and in higher positions of authority and responsibility, I must say that I know of no way of forcing the Services to cut administrative and overhead cost to the bone except by arbitrary action. This does not mean that I would support every move that Mr. Johnson has made, although I understand that he has several times referred to his current proposals as the "Eisenhower Budget." Last spring when I was in Washington, my job was to propose a division of the available money, under varying assumptions as to quantity, so as to carry out as nearly as we possibly could the essentials of the agreed upon strategic plan. This says a very great deal in a relatively short sentence. Particularly, it says a lot in the way of difficult problems. My experiences in the attempt to achieve some success are far too long and involved for me to attempt to describe them in anything less than a full Volume. But I would be quite ready to wager that, if I could send to you the full record of all of the efforts that were made, of all the different types of approaches that were used, and could show you the responses received from each of the Services, you would agree that the answers recommended were about as logical and as nearly correct as any individual could make them. Such a wager I would make with some confidence because of the fact that I kept pounding away until the actual percentages of the total budget—that had to be allocated on my judgment (that is, outside the roughly agreed upon conclusions of all three Services)—were extremely small. While I am relying upon a weakening memory, I am quite certain that, even in the smallest of the several budgets on which we worked, the percentage could not have been more than three or, at the very maximum, four. So you will see that from my viewpoint the heat and intensity that characterized the quarrel were unjustified and evidenced to me a flagrant failure to place national convictions and requirements above those of Service.

I realize that I have never before attempted to explain some of these things to you in such detail. I would probably be even more explicit in this particular exposition except for the obvious requirements of secrecy in all of the deliberations and functioning of the Chiefs of Staff and of their relationships with their civilian superiors. But I should like you to believe that there are many sides to this whole argument and it has been a weary battle to get men to forget self and to turn their minds to the critical situation in the world and to think of nothing else. It is because I believe that Sherman possesses a sensitive and logical concern for the national picture, as opposed to any more narrow one, that I spoke so warmly of his appointment. He has, so far as I know, both the ability to do the job and the will to do it properly. Each of these qualifications is extraordinarily important in this day and time.

Along with a letter of such length must come my profound apology, but I just felt today like attempting to give you a fuller explanation of some of the events of the past, and of which I have some knowledge, than I have given you before.

As a sort of postscript to the above, I must tell you that I agree with your opinion that no personal aide should be with any General too long. For this reason, as much as I appreciate his services and as grateful as I am to him, I have constantly urged my present aide to transfer to other duties. Moreover, no one has ever been on my personal staff for one single second except by his own preference. The only thing that I have not done is to insist upon a transfer against the expressed desire of the individual concerned. I must remark also that where you recalled the length of my service with MacArthur at 5 years, you should have used the figure "9."

As ever,

Capt. John G. Crommelin, Jr., had been a principal figure in the "revolt of the admirals" during the fall of 1949 and was subsequently disciplined for his role in the affair. He continued to attack the administration, however, and became increasingly active in right-wing politics. In 1954 he would help lead a petition drive on behalf of Sen. Joseph R. McCarthy. "That bozo should be given the silent treatment," wrote Swede on 14 March 1950.

---

20 March 1950

Dear Swede:

Had I known that I could possibly have impressed you so much with one miniature typewriter, I would have sent you one a long time ago.

I am sorry to hear that you and Ibby have had this virus pneumonia. Mamie's father had a siege of it when he was visiting us this winter and I think it was only this new drug, aureomycin (possibly that is nearly correct), which pulled him through. This note brings my fervent hope that you both are well again.

I cannot recall the man from Abilene named [Walter] Alexander. Your story of the love life of his father left me a bit amazed; I did not realize that we had an Abilenite who was so light-footed and light-hearted as to jump out of one matrimonial venture in order to get tangled up with a senorita. It must have been the Naval influence!

I was interested to read your observations about Crommelin. By the way, you may have seen an account of one incident that occurred just after he reached San Francisco. (If I told you about this in a former letter, just please skip it here.) He asked for a press conference and talked rather wildly about a "Prussian General Staff in the Pentagon." Apparently failing to stir up comment as he had hoped, he finally fired a gun which he hoped would be of really big caliber. It was something about as follows: "I am particularly disturbed that a man in uniform who is definitely a candidate for the Presidency, but who will not announce his allegiance to either political party, is free both to influence decisions within the Pentagon and to present his views to the Congress." There was a bit more to the story, as reported to me by Forrest Sherman, but that will give you some idea of the fantastic lengths to which the man goes in order to attract attention. I think

76

that you understand, as clearly as anyone else, that I have gone to the Pentagon or to the Congress only when ordered or insistently requested to do so. Moreover, I have constantly pled that we should forget the quarrels of the past and, particularly, the attempt to fix blame for unfortunate outbursts. I have constantly urged that we turn our attention to the future on the basis of *mutual cooperation and understanding.* Crommelin, I think, cannot fail to know this as well as anybody else. But I think, also, that he has gotten so avid for acclaim and headlines that he will say anything in order to achieve that purpose.

With respect to the handling of the case, I must say that I feel sorry for the Navy, particularly for Sherman. While it has been my practice always to ignore this type of thing and so deny to the offender the opportunity to appear as a martyr, yet there finally comes a point where the very good name of the Navy (or any other Service in which such an incident occurs) is involved. The country expects its Armed Services to be models of discipline and deportment and the spectacle of successful insubordination is one to create fear in the minds of the public that their traditions of service and subordination to civilian authority are deteriorating. It seems to me to be another case of "whether you do or whether you don't, you are bound to regret it."

No one respects courage and gallantry in battle more than I do. Goodness knows that I have had more reason than most people to be eternally grateful that in a pinch a young American exhibits an extraordinary disregard for the dangers of the battlefield. Nevertheless, I feel that we cannot, in succeeding years of peace, constantly excuse, condone and ignore serious offenses committed by individuals, whether civilian or military, merely because their physical courage has been established beyond a doubt.

These are merely observations—I have no exact knowledge of any kind applying to this case, and my information is based entirely on what the newspapers have said and what Forrest Sherman has told me. Incidentally, Forrest called me to apologize for what he called "an unwarranted attack on one of the Navy's friends." Personally, the whole thing bothers me not a whit; I don't believe I have mentioned it to anyone but you. But I repeat that my sympathy is with those who have to handle such disagreeable cases.

With respect to young [Alvin] Wingfield, I will, on your suggestion, always be glad to see him. However, he should be careful to telephone or otherwise communicate with my office (Mr. [Kevin] McCann, UNiversity 4-3200, Ext. 2773) well in advance of the proposed visit so that we can find a free period and set up the engagement.

Love to Ibby and, as always, warmest regards to you,

As ever,

War began in late June 1950, when North Korea invaded South Korea and President Truman committed the United States on the side of the South Koreans. Eisenhower strongly supported the president's decision, though he was critical of the administration's failure to mobilize more rapidly. He was also more critical of administration defense policies than he had been only a few months earlier. By September, when he wrote this letter, the fighting had temporarily stabilized along the "Pusan perimeter" on the southern tip of the peninsula. Three days later General MacArthur launched a daring amphibious landing at Inchon, some two hundred miles behind enemy lines. United Nations forces quickly rolled back the North Koreans and then pressed ahead, determined to crush the North Korean army and unify the peninsula under American auspices. This action, which Eisenhower had joined other American leaders in advocating, led to Chinese intervention and to an expanded and prolonged war.

---

12 September 1950

Dear Swede:

This will probably be a very short letter but this does not mean that I fail to appreciate every single paragraph and sentence of your fine missive of August 9th. Of course I am delighted that you liked my "Silver" lecture. I worked like a dog on it, during the odd moments of several weeks. Recently I have had to give another talk and again I worked the same way. This latest one, which I delivered on Labor Day, was even more difficult to prepare than the long one that you read. This was because I wanted to say a very great deal in twelve and one-half minutes. To undertake such a chore without allowing the text to become nothing more than a disjointed collection of empty platitudes and aphorisms is rather difficult for an old soldier. During the last days of my ordeal of preparation, I had a couple of friends come to visit me to help out. I am certainly lucky in the friends I have. These two had to come from a considerable distance, interrupting their own vacations, yet they came just as if it were fun to do it.

It is slightly irritating to learn that your typewriter is showing some defectiveness in operation. I remember when I told [Maj. Robert L.] Schulz to procure one of them, I told him I wanted one that was noted for its durability and for its general excellence in operation. I hope you will telephone the man who delivered it to you and give him instructions to get on the job with necessary repairs.

The Korean situation seems to be in something of a stalemate over the past several weeks. Most of us are puzzled by some of the developments and certainly all of us are experiencing a definite feeling of frustration. However, we should not fall into the slovenly and easily acquired habit of just blaming others for all our misfortunes. However, it seems quite clear that, in one particular, the civilian authorities of our government must take a very considerable share of blame. They have never been very seriously impressed by professional insistence upon the permanent mainte-nance of a "task force" or as it is sometimes called, a "striking force." It has always been obvious that a democracy, even one as rich as ours, could not maintain in peace the force in being that could promptly and successfully meet any trouble that might arise in any portion of the globe, particularly if such trouble should occur simultaneoulsy in two or three places. But the existence of a fine, properly balanced, effectively commanded and reasonably strong task force would not only have a deterrent effect upon potential enemies, but would give us a splendid "fire department" basis on which to meet actual aggression.

Beyond all this, however, we must recognize that we, in America, have never liked to face up to the problem arising out of the conflicting considerations of national security on the one hand and economic and financial solvency on the other. We have always felt a long ways removed from any potential and powerful enemy. Our experience has given us the feeling that we have available a cushion of space that would provide, automatically, a similar cushion of time. Consequently, we have not pondered deeply over the individual's obligations to the State, which provides to him protection in his way of life, nor have we been compelled to consider how the discharge of these obligations could most effectively and economically be accomplished.

During World War II, I was so frequently shocked and dismayed by the results of the incomplete training of our youth and by their lack of knowledge of the age-old struggle between individual freedom and dictatorship, that I came, unthinkingly, to assume that after the war our people would at last meet all these issues head on and do something effective about them. As a consequence, all of my thinking during the latter part of the war was based upon the assumption that America would adopt at the war's end some system of universal military *service*, a system whereby every young man would be required to give some 18 months of his time to the government and that the professional element of our security force would, therefore, be held to a minimum. Since such service would, I thought, be performed in discharge of an obligation, there would be no pay other than that for maintenance and a very small monetary allowance. I likewise thought that we would develop means and methods of producing the munitions of war, including stockpiling, without profit to anyone.

In these assumptions I was, of course, proved quite wrong. When I came home, General Marshall told me that we could certainly get no more than a program of universal military training and that it would take a lot of work to put even this compromise across. I took his advice—especially when I found that the President was already sold on this idea—and worked hard for the UMT program. We were defeated even though I am still convinced that the great mass of our people definitely favor the proposition. I am sure that if the law had been passed some of our National Guard divisions would have, before this, been ready to leave for Korea.

With respect to your speculation that Germany may be the next place in which internecine warfare will break out, I should like to observe that if this should be the case, then Russia would, thereby, come very close to declaring open, all out, war. This is because of the fact that *her* troops are in actual occupation of Eastern Germany and in actual *control* of that area. Consequently, if she allows them to move to the attack, she cannot possibly longer hide behind the subterfuge that a "people's government" is attempting to liberate their brothers in another part of the country.

I shall not be able to get down to Gordon Gray's inauguration. The early part of October is already filled with so many engagements on my calendar that I am seriously thinking of going to the hospital for a week or so. I should like to be at his installation—more to have a long talk with you than to attend another ceremony. This is true in spite of the fact that I like Gordon Gray immensely and I am delighted that he is taking over a job that he is going to find a great deal tougher than he suspects.

My love to Ibby and the children.

Cordially,

In late October 1950 President Truman summoned Eisenhower to the White House and asked him to become supreme commander of NATO forces in Europe. Only Eisenhower's great prestige and diplomatic skill, Truman and other leaders in the administration believed, would assuage French fears over German rearmament and permit the creation of an integrated military force in western Europe. Eisenhower agreed to take the post, as indeed his sense of duty dictated, though he was clearly reluctant to do so.

Dear Swede:

I am returning to you the partially written letter that Mr. [Louis] Graves sent to you some time back. Whenever I read such convincing evidence that I am held high in the esteem of a loyal and obviously thoughtful American, I experience a feeling that I cannot possibly describe. More than likely, it is a combination of a clear realization of my own unworthiness of such an opinion, but this mingled with an equal sentiment of pride.

As to conclusions concerning my future responsibility and duty, I think you know my ideas on this perfectly well. Moreover, the longer I live the more I realize that no individual can predict with confidence anything concerning "tomorrow." At this moment I am confronted with possibilities of profound import; possibilities that had not even crossed my mind as much as a month ago. You yourself mention them in your handwritten note on Mr. Graves' manuscript. You say, "I do hope that this weekend you won't be talked into that Atlantic Pact job."

I am a little astonished at your use of the expression, "talked into." As you know, I am an officer on the active list on which I will always stay, by reason of a special Act of Congress, affecting a few of us, unless I voluntarily remove myself from it. It is clear that my official superiors don't have to do any talking if they actually want me to take any military assignment.

But over and above such considerations and addressing myself to the merits of the case, I would conclude from your statement that you do not attach the same importance to the success of the Atlantic Defense Pact as I do. I rather look upon this effort as about the last remaining chance for the survival of Western civilization. Our efforts in the United Nations have been defeated by the vetoes of hostile groups—but in the Atlantic Pact we are not plagued by the hostile groups and are simply trying to work out a way that free countries may band together to protect themselves. If we allow the whole plan to fizzle out into a miserable failure, it would seem to me that our future would be bleak indeed.

Of course, if the authorities can find anyone else who will tackle the job, and who they believe can perform it, then I hasten to agree with you that that man would probably do it far better than I could. Moreover, I believe, in my present job, I am supporting an effort that will be of unusual significance to the welfare of our people. But I still would not agree that there is any job in the world today that is more important than getting Atlantic Union defensive forces and arrangements off to a good, practical and speedy start.

Of course, all this may be meaningless; I do not want or need any other job. Moreover, I understand from the morning's paper that the [NATO] Council in Washington seems further than ever from agreement. But the matter still retains its grave importance and so long as it does, anyone of us—no matter what his station, his position or what personal sacrifices might be involved—must be ready to do his best.

As ever,

1951

Eisenhower wrote a brief note to Swede in early February 1951, when he returned from an exploratory tour of European capitals. In April he formally assumed command of Supreme Headquarters Allied Powers Europe (SHAPE), and by June, when he wrote this letter, he was deeply involved in the politics of the North Atlantic Treaty Organization. In his letter of June 1, Swede noted that ''the country is sitting back, perhaps too complacently, in the comfortable belief that Ike has everything in hand in Europe.''

---

21 June 1951

Dear Swede:

Recently, I have been wondering when I was to get another letter from you; a question that was finally answered by your letter dated June 1.

Trying to make some comment on each subject you raise— and, God knows, my observations will not only have to be limited, but will possibly be better classified as hazy day-dreaming—I start out by saying that, if anyone thinks this whole task is ''comfortably in hand,'' he had better acquaint himself a little more accurately with facts as they are. How can anyone in the world believe that numbers of nations could, within a short space of months, so organize, develop, and train themselves that they were even capable of putting out timely and necessary decisions in such a matter as mutual defense, to say nothing of accomplishing all the material, mental, and psychological jobs as are included? Time and effort and understanding, and renewed effort and tireless study, and still more effort, would comprise a fair recipe for the product we are trying to obtain.

There are, of course, certain encouraging developments. I am quite sure that anyone acquainted with Europe would, as of now, sense a tremendous increase in morale, courage, and determination as compared to the level of these only six months to a year ago. On every front, there has been some improvement, even though progress is far less rapid than we could wish or even have the right, in certain instances, to expect.

The one indispensable thing to remember is that, if the free world cannot provide for its "collective" security, the alternative for every one of these nations, including our own, is an eventual fate that is worse than any kind of expense or effort we can now imagine. Consequently, American leadership must be exerted every minute of the day, every day, to make sure that we are securing from these combined countries their maximum of accomplishment. Where any nation fails—as some of them are, of course, partially failing now—we must take a certain portion of the responsibility by admitting that, in that particular instance, our leadership has been partially ineffective.

I assure you that, as I go around to various capitals and meet with members of the several governments, I never let up for one single instant on pounding home some serious facts. The first of these is that each country must provide the heart and soul of its own defense. If the heart is right, other nations can help; if not, that particular nation is doomed. Morale cannot be imported.

Next, I insist that Europe must, as a whole, provide in the long run for its own defense. The United States can move in and, by its psychological, intellectual, and material leadership, help to produce arms, units, and the confidence that will allow Europe to solve its problem. In the long run, it is not possible—and most certainly not desirable—that Europe should be an occupied territory defended by legions brought in from abroad, somewhat in the fashion that Rome's territories vainly sought security many hundred years ago.

To my mind, Turkey and Greece are nations that must be brought into our defensive structure very definitely and soon.[1] Whether or not they should be militarily attached to my command, or should be divided—possibly with Greece under our particular umbrella and Turkey under another—are problems that are susceptible of several solutions. The main thing is that they, with us, should make common cause against a common enemy and make this job one of top priority in each country.

As to Iran, I think the whole thing is tragic.[2] A stream of visitors goes through my office, and some of the individuals concerned seem to consider themselves as authorities on the Iranian question. Numbers of them attach as much blame to Western stupidity as to Iranian fanaticism and Communist intrigue in bringing about all the trouble. Frankly, I have gotten to the point that I am concerned primarily, and almost solely, in some scheme or plan that will permit that oil to keep flowing to the westward. We cannot ignore the tremendous importance of 675,000 barrels of oil a day. The situation there has not yet gotten into as bad a position as China, but sometimes I think it stands today at the same place that China did only a very few years ago. Now we have completely lost the latter nation—no matter how we explain it, how much we prove our position to have been fair and just, we *failed*. I most certainly hope that this calamity is not repeated in the case of Iran.

So far as all the MacArthur-Korean-administration-partisan politics affair is concerned, I have kept my mouth closed in every

1. In deference to the concerns of other European nations, neither Greece nor Turkey had originally been included in NATO. Administration thinking changed, however, after the beginning of the Korean War, and in February 1951 the National Security Council had recommended the inclusion of both in the Western alliance. The formal invitation to join would come the next year.
2. In May 1951 Iran's nationalist prime minister, Mohammed Mossadegh, won parliamentary approval to nationalize the holdings of the giant British-owned Anglo-Iranian Oil Company. In retaliation, Anglo-Iranian and the other large oil companies that dominated international petroleum markets declared a boycott on all Iranian oil, thereby hoping to bring the Iranian government to its knees. Their efforts failed, however, as did attempts by the United States and other countries to mediate the dispute. In 1953 Eisenhower, then president, directed the CIA to help overthrow Mossadegh and to replace him with the young Shah Mohammed Reza Pahlavi.

language of which I have ever heard.[3] I have some very definite views about parts of the sorry mess, but I do not have a sufficiently clear picture of the whole development, starting with some of the machinations and incidents of World War II, to allow me to make up my mind on many of the important features of the affair. I guess that the most we can hope out of the thing is that soon the Communists will quit pushing the conflict (terminating it somewhat as they did the attacks on Greece), and that we succeed in developing a sufficient strength among the South Koreans to withdraw the vast bulk of our own forces.

[Gen. Albert C.] Wedemeyer's testimony left me in complete bewilderment as I attempted to follow his reasoning. Moreover, I am not quite sure what *you* mean when you talk about "punishing the aggressor." Unless you can get at Mao and the small group of advisers he has right around him, I do not believe we would be punishing the aggressor merely by bombing Canton, Shanghai, or any other place where we would most certainly be killing a number of our friends along with the people who are true followers of the Communists.

I will not comment at all upon your observations concerning your dilemma in the next election if you have to vote for either of the two men you name [Truman and Ohio Republican Robert A. Taft]. With respect to your statement, "Worse luck, you seem to be pretty well out of the present picture," I wish I could feel that way as definitely as you do. Not only has there been a very recent poll taken which continues to stir up trouble, but a whole bevy of visitors here, and correspondents in the States, keep plugging away at a contrary view and determination.

I never heard of Clugston [who had written a right-wing attack entitled *Eisenhower for President?*]. Moreover, I am told that his book was written as a very sly piece of "smear" work. I can't be bothered, although he is one campaigner who is apparently in league with another fellow named Dewey Taft who publishes a

3. Truman had relieved the insubordinate General MacArthur of command in Korea in April 1951, triggering a torrent of criticism. Although privately critical of MacArthur, Eisenhower heeded the advice of his old friend Gen. Lucius D. Clay, who warned him to "let no one maneuver you into any . . . comment on the MacArthur incident."

queer little paper down in Wichita. This latter character insists that I am one of the great friends of Communism in our country, and the darling of Moscow. I wish to God he could see some of the propaganda spread around this country by the Communist Party. If I am not Moscow's number one public enemy today, then I am certainly running that number one man a close race.

You are right in your idea that I had nothing to do with the appointment of [Adm. William M.] Fechteler [the new naval commander for NATO], but you are wrong that I went over backward in naming Monty [Field Marshal Bernard L. Montgomery, one of Eisenhower's old antagonists] as my Deputy. Monty not only has a very fine reputation in this region as a soldier, but *he is one*. Moreover, he is a very determined little fellow who knows exactly what he wants, is simple and direct in his approach, and minces no words with any soldier, politician, or plain citizen when he thinks that that particular individual (or the country he represents) is not fulfilling his complete obligations to NATO. He is one man who clearly recognizes the truth of the assertion that Europe cannot forever depend upon America for military and economic aid and assistance. He hammers away at the idea that this region must become self-sufficient.

We shall be on the look-out for your friend Corydon Lyons. If he brings along his students, I think I shall be secretly a bit on the pleased side. Sometimes I get quite weary of talking to the old, the fearful, and the cautious. I like to meet young people with their fresh outlook and their fixed, even if sometimes too complacent, assumption that they can meet the problems of their own time.

It was nice to hear that Bob Baughey [an air force public-relations officer and mutual friend] had been to see you. Not long ago, I had a letter from him.

I assure you that we are not enjoying Paris in the sense that we would prefer to be here instead of in the United States. I think that, if ever two people have had enough of foreign service, we are they. We look forward to coming home—not the least of our pleasures will be a visit with you and Ibby. In the meantime, please keep writing.

Cordially,

In a handwritten note on August 22, Swede enclosed a letter by his friend and essayist Harold W. Whicker on the theme of painting. "As I've told you before, Whick is a he-man—ex-professional wrestler, English prof, outstanding painter and essayist, outdoorsman—who is afflicted with a heart ailment but doesn't let it get him down."

4 September 1951

Dear Swede:

It has been a long time since I last read one of the letters you receive periodically from Whicker. Yet that interval is not so long that I fail to recall at once the primary emotion his writing always inspires in me—a feeling that here is one man who is able to put down in print a clear expression of the thoughts that flow through his brain as he contemplates the beauty of a sylvan scene, the capabilities of man for sacrifice, and the exceedingly disappointing result we seem always to get when we find men attempting to act as a group in the solution of common political and social problems. He finds ways and means of describing, with cameo-like sharpness, his disappointment that men respond far more easily to a selfish impulse than to a noble one; he is so convincing in this regard that his reader (this one at least) comes to feel that the conclusion as to relativity—wheat to chaff—is a gross overstatement.

Of course, I am intrigued by his explanation of his reasons for painting. You may or may not know that I indulge in the same habit. But in my case there is no faintest semblance of talent, and certainly I paint for far less complicated or worthy reasons than does Mr. Whicker. Some years ago I found that I had to limit my hours devoted to serious and steady reading; my life is given over to such incessant contemplation of heavy and weighty problems—most of them made more difficult by the circumstances that they have no final and complete answer—that some kind of release or relief became necessary in order to keep me up to the bit and operating at reasonable efficiency during the hours when I deal in the affairs for which I bear some responsibility. So I took up painting. I did it without a lesson and I have persisted in it for more than three years with no more constructive help from the outside than an occasional piece of casual criticism from one of my artist friends. For me the real benefit is the fact that it gives me an excuse to be absolutely alone and interferes not at all with what I am pleased to call my "contemplative powers." In other words, I paint for fun, for recreation, for enjoyment. When the work is woefully bad, so that even I recognize its stupidity or banality, I merely turn it upside down and start again. After I do this often enough I burn that particular canvas. But once in awhile one comes out so that it is definitely better than I know how to do! That one I keep. Such a one may be a portrait, a picture of a tree, or merely a colored sketch of a couple of flowers. The point is that one with no talent, no ability to draw and no time to waste can get a lot of fun out of daubing with oils. Most of mine is done between the hours of 11 and 12 at night, but when the effort I am making seems worthwhile pursuing in daylight, then I have a fine early Sunday morning pastime.

All this to tell you how much I really envy your friend's ability to paint in a way that pleases himself and the time to do it.

I like his facility of expression—even his flow of words. His style reflects not only an appreciation of niceties and of nuances, but his unhurried and even wordy way of reaching his conclusions adds confidence, because it implies that he had time to think the matter through carefully. I am tempted to believe he is right in the suggestion that to attain sheer personal happiness one ought, through some judgment accepted by all, be relegated, inexorably, to a life in a woodland cottage.

As to his conclusions about the American scene, I most thoroughly concur in his condemnation of public violators of the principles of decency and honor. Now, none of us is so strong that he is spared the painful embarrassment of looking back upon moments of weakness; none is so wise that he cannot recall times when his own ignorance bordered upon the stupid, even the moronic. Nevertheless, high standards must be upheld—he helps to do so! He beautifully expresses his respect for courage, integrity and honest effort.

Some day I should like to spend a week with him, just sitting in his backyard and possibly talking about nothing more removed than the trees and the mountains that he loves so well.

My love to Ibby and your nice family and, as always, my very best to you.

Cordially,

P.S. I see that you wrote your letter in longhand. Did the blankety-blank typewriter play out? The reason I ask is a bit more than a mere concern for your convenience; I was told that the particular typewriter we got was the sturdiest and best in its field. If it wasn't, I would like to write a sarcastic letter to the producing firm.

By the autumn of 1951 the pressure on Eisenhower to announce his candidacy for the presidency had become intense. During the summer a group of his business friends had organized, with his tacit approval, Citizens for Eisenhower; and soon Eisenhower for President clubs were springing up all around the country. The steady stream of business and political leaders coursing through his headquarters in Paris increased, as did his private correspondence. In a front-page editorial in the *New York Herald Tribune*, his friend William Robinson endorsed him for the Republican nomination. It seems clear that Eisenhower was himself moving closer and closer to a declaration of candidacy; and in his correspondence with friends and supporters, as in the ensuing letter to Swede, he was careful to distinguish his own position from both the liberalism of the Truman administration and the extreme conservatism of the Taft Republicans. "Almost daily I'm asked whether or not you'll run," wrote Swede on November 2. "Invariably I answer that I know you don't want it but that you will, as always, answer a call to duty as your conscience hears it— that if you feel you are necessary to the nation's welfare you'll get into the race." For Eisenhower's confirmation, see paragraph thirteen below.

Dear Swede:

Thank goodness, you relieved my mind about the durability and efficiency of the Royal—until I received your reassuring letter, I had the unhappy feeling that Schulz may have been taken for a ride in the purchase he made.

One of the infrequent chuckles that I have had in recent days was inspired by your sentence that "I see so much in the papers about Eisenhower these days that I sometimes wonder if I really know the man they are writing about." If *you* think that, what do you suppose I feel? I find in the Communist press that I am a bloody Fascist, a war monger, and a tool of American Imperialists. The cartoons that accompany these accounts picture a big-paunched, heavy-jawed Germanic type of brutal soldier. At the same time, I find somewhat similar cartoons in sections of our Isolationist press, but in which the labels assert that I am a great friend of Joe Stalin's or of all the Internationalist do-gooders in the world. In one paper, I am a New Dealer; in the next, I am such a Reactionary that the CIO [Congress of Industrial Organizations] finds it necessary to condemn me as an economic anachronism. In the eyes of one columnist, I am too fearful and frightened ever to attempt to fill a political office; another columnist asserts that I am, with Machiavellian cunning, pulling every possible string to become President of the United States.

All this is ordinary fare for anyone who tries to pursue a steady and honest course down the only path available when he is dealing in complex activities pertaining to large organizations of humans—a path straight down the middle of the road. Sometime in September of 1949, I think it was, I made a talk before the National Bar Association, then meeting in Saint Louis. I pointed out that anyone who chose the middle of the road was going constantly to be subject to attack from both extremes. He is hated by the bureaucrats and the national planners, and he is distrusted by those who think that Calvin Coolidge was a pink. All of which would be rather terrifying to the victim if it were anything new or unique; actually, it is nothing but a mere repetition of what has been happening for hundreds, even thousands, of years.

You and I have had earlier correspondence concerning our common admiration for Forrest Sherman. So you must know how bitterly I regret his death. To my mind, there was no real second to him and, as I recall, I wrote you one letter stoutly defending his selection as Chief of Naval Operations when I thought you had expressed some doubt about the matter. I do remember, though, that you wrote me a later letter to say that I had misunderstood the statements in which I thought I had found the criticisms.

With respect to the top Service jobs in Washington, I believe that our people have, as yet, a lot to learn. For the Joint Chiefs of Staff to coordinate and balance the great military organisms that our country needs in these days of tension requires, in each member, selflessness, energy, study, and the broadest kind of viewpoint and comprehension. Each of these men must cease regarding himself as the advocate or special pleader for any particular Service; he must think strictly and solely in terms of the United States. Character rather than intellect, and moral courage rather than mere professional skill, are the dominant qualifications required. Each individual will have to give only a modicum of his time to the establishment of policy affecting his own Service, because his great problem will be how to work with two others in devising and recommending to the civilian authorities a properly balanced force together with the programs and methods that should be applied to the problem of building global security for ourselves.

If you were choosing the Chief of Naval Operations by application of the standards I have just alluded to, I do not know where your choice would fall. I am not well acquainted with some of the men now coming to the front in the Navy, but there is one whom you did *not* mention and who, on short acquaintance, has impressed me greatly. He is the Vice Chief of Naval Operations, named [Adm. Donald B.] Duncan. He is quiet, almost self-effacing, but he seems to me to have a value that far exceeds the noise that he makes. Just as I always felt that there was no one in uniform who loomed above Sherman in value to our country, so I have some suspicion that Duncan may finally make a similar impression upon me. (Not, of course, that this is important but, after all, our correspondence is a personal thing, and so I find no need to apologize for my personal views.) I believe [Adm. William M.] Fechteler will do a good job [as chief of naval operations]—just possibly an outstanding one, because he seems to have a disposition that is neither easily upset nor particularly upsetting to others. He is one of those people who does not make the mistake of confusing strength and bad manners.

[Adm. Robert B.] Carney, of course, is a very skillful and able person. I think at times that he may be tempted to argue points rather legalistically and, because of this tendency, may give unwarranted importance to minor detail. I think this is subconscious but it does, on occasion, give his presentations an atmosphere of contentiousness. However, he is saved from any really bad effects because of his general popularity with his associates—all of us like him. He is most courteous and hospitable.

Incidentally, when I was in the Mediterranean recently, I renewed friendship with Admiral [Matthias B.] Gardner, I suppose of the Class of '17 or '18. I like him very much and have a great respect for his easy-going but effective methods.

Your letter brought me my first news that there had been any public intimation that even one, much less two, Eisenhowers were considered for the job of Baseball Commissioner. Over the past several years, informal suggestions of this character have been made to me, but my refusals to consider the matter have been both prompt and emphatic. This has not meant that I was insensible to the compliment implicit in the suggestion, but it has meant that it is not the kind of work in which I felt it best for me to engage. I had no idea that the job had ever been suggested to Milton, but I am quite sure that, if it was, his reaction was somewhat the same.

I feel impelled to pause for just a moment to make an observation concerning the topsy-turvy happenings that we accept, today, almost as commonplaces. If, some forty-five years ago, anyone had suggested to two barefoot boys of the Dickinson County region that they would one day casually—without even a second thought—dismiss an opportunity to take over an honorable and decent job paying $75,000 a year, the entire countryside would have, at that moment, broken into a very hearty laugh, not to mention a few snorts of derision. But that's the way it goes! I am not so terribly much richer in money than I was in those days (even though we had nothing then) but I guess that, in certain respects, my sense of values has changed considerably. And, after all, anyone with a $75,000 salary must have a great deal of anguish when he figures out his income tax!

The West Point scandal [in which a number of cadets were caught cheating] made me heartsick. The only grain of comfort I get out of the whole business was that apparently the authorities, when aroused to the knowledge that something incompatible with the honor system was going on, met the problem head on and without equivocation.

One single observation about Korea-Iran-Egypt-Germany-and all the other spots on the earth in which we now sometimes find ourselves embarrassed. They are all part and parcel of the same great struggle—the struggle of free men to govern themselves effectively and efficiently; to protect themselves from any threat without, and to prevent their system from collapsing under them, due to the strains placed upon it by their defensive effort. It is another phase of a struggle that has been going on for some three thousand years; the unique feature about it now is that it is much more than ever before a single worldwide conflict with power polarized in the two centers of Washington and Moscow.

There is no point in my commenting further upon the political questions that you mention and with which I am so often personally confronted. Your own analysis remains accurate so far as I can foresee the future.

When I am attempting to answer letters from inquiring friends on the point, I normally include in the explanation of my own attitude a paragraph about as follows:

"For me to admit, while in this post, a partisan political loyalty would properly be resented by thinking Americans and would be doing a disservice to our country. Such action on my part would encourage partisan thinking, in our country, toward a job in which the whole nation has already invested tremendous sums. The successful outcome of this venture is too vital to our welfare in the years head to permit any semblance of partisan allegiance on the part of the United States Military Commander in SHAPE."

I believe that a bit of reflection will establish that there is no other possible course for me as long as I am in uniform. A man cannot desert a duty, but it would seem that he could lay down one in order to pick up a heavier and more responsible burden. So far as personal desire or ambition is concerned, there will *never* be any change for me. I could not be more negative.

I am glad you told me about the word "exegete." I am now going to look it up in the dictionary before I go home.

My love to your nice family.

Cordially,

1952

Although Eisenhower, as we have seen, had moved steadily closer to a declaration of candidacy, he remained unwilling to commit himself completely, either publicly or in his private correspondence. This was particularly frustrating for supporters such as Sen. Henry Cabot Lodge, who believed that if Eisenhower were to win the nomination, he would have to declare his candidacy and return home—"possibly, I suppose, as a deserter," Eisenhower wryly observed. Eisenhower's reasons for holding back were complex. He was genuinely ambivalent about running, and he was especially reluctant to commit himself to what he viewed as the distasteful task of campaigning for delegates. But he also shrewdly understood the appeal of a candidate who appeared to stand above partisan politics—couldn't "something of a virtue be made . . . of my refusal to have my attention diverted from my assigned duty?" he asked. And though he allowed Lodge and others to campaign hard on his behalf throughout early 1952, he was determined not to return until June, when, as his close friend Lucius Clay put it, "you will be a fresh figure, untouched by all the campaigning that is now going on, and a certain Republican winner."

12 February 1952

Dear Swede:

The first paragraph of your letter mentions a prescribed periodicity of three months for your letters. I just want to remind you that the prescription is self-imposed.

It was a bit amusing to find that you had also been puzzled by some of the statements made in Mr. Harger's *American Magazine* article [on Eisenhower's appointment to West Point] two or three months back. Such errors as appear in it, however, mean to me only that the human memory is a frail, not to say a treacherous, thing. The older one grows, the more noticeable this is—I have certainly gotten to the point where I don't like to be too positive about commonplace occurrences of 40 years ago. However, in this case, the occurrence was far from commonplace for me—even though it was for most of the people of Abilene and, for them, remained so until the day arrived when my name began to appear with astonishing frequency in the newspapers. It was simply too big a gap for their memories to bridge and to make the far end come out at exactly the point where it originally lay.

However, there is this about Mr. Harger. Speaking roughly, he is about the only one left who was, in 1910, prominent in Abilene affairs. This statement, of course, excepts Charlie Case, but at that particular moment he was over-shadowed, to say the least, by his dad. As the years have rolled on and those who worked so hard for my appointment have died, Mr. Harger has become almost my sole contact with that particular generation of Abilene citizens. Consequently, he has rather symbolized for me the 1910 kindness of the whole community, and in my conversations and correspondence with him, the recipient of my genuine gratitude toward the whole community. Actually—if you will recall—the man who appointed me was one of the earliest so-called "Progressives," Senator Joseph Bristow. Mr. Harger was in the other branch of the Republican Party, in those days called the "Stand patters." As a consequence of this situation, Mr. P. [Phil] W. Heath was the spearhead of my supporting phalanx. Others were Mr. [Reynold G.] Rogers, Mr. [Alfred M.] Ward (a jeweler), the Hurds [brothers Arthur and Bruce], Mr. [Henry C.] Litts, and dozens of others who wrote letters to the Senator in my behalf. Among these, of course, Mr. Harger was included. But I repeat that, so far as I am concerned, and *as of to-day*, he is the solely responsible individual (except for yourself, from whom I derived both confidence and inspiration).

I am not particularly amazed that you have had no answer to the letter you sent to Senator Lodge. You must remember that he and his associates are busy politicians and have had little real opportunity, so far, to organize an office in which to do all the work that they apparently expect to perform. I am quite certain that neither Senator Lodge nor any of his associates would deliberately ignore such an offer as you made. I am sure that he personally is one of those who clearly discerns the need for organization, but he would require time in which to build it. All this is written without the benefit of any personal knowledge of what is going on. But I do know Cabot Lodge to be a very courteous, keen, and knowledge-able Senator, so I feel sure that my explanation is correct (and, of course, possibly your letter to him was lost).

Your professorial luncheon partner was not particularly origi-nal in accusing me of "coyness." The charge is repeated in some form or another in every day's mail. It causes me no distress—this for the reason that I occupy the enviable position of a man who wants nothing. It does cause me a bit of amazement that many people who regard themselves as enlightened and well-educated simply cannot get it into their heads that there may be some individuals who still regard the word "duty" as a governing one in their lives. Only a handful of my correspondents, including yourself, give me credit for meaning exactly what I say and are completely sympathetic with my attitude. Even among this tiny group, a few still believe that there is something more that I should do immediately in the political arena. They argue that I could do so without, in any way, violating my determination to avoid par-ticipation in the preconvention campaign.

The general run of such recommendations roll off my back like water from a duck. But when the occasional one comes from tried and true friends, I get to wondering whether I am a bit stiff-necked in adhering to my own opinions. I haven't any complete answer at this moment. All that you can be sure of is that, barring unforeseen and extraordinary circumstances, I shall not do anything that I personally feel should be interpreted as "preconvention political activities."

Last evening, Mamie and I saw a showing of a film made at the "Eisenhower Rally" at Madison Square Garden. It was brought over here by Jacqueline Cochran, who was one of the co-chairmen of the demonstration. The New York show was held at midnight, and according to Miss Cochran, with the obstacle of a very non-cooperative police and fire department. Nevertheless, she said that the crowd, which had been predicted by the police department to reach not more than four thousand, included at its height about thirty-three thousand people. She said that a blunder of the fire department kept some four thousand of these from coming inside the hall. In any event, the two hour film brought home to me for the first time something of the depth of the longing in America today for change—a change that would bring, they hope, some confidence that the disturbing problems of our country will be sensibly attacked and progress made toward solving them. I can't tell you what an emotional upset it is for one to realize suddenly that he himself may become the symbol of that longing and hope. Possibly I would not have been so impressed had the demonstration been planned over a period of months, and put on at a reasonable hour.

I never forget America's great need for success in the job of building collective security in that part of the world still outside of the Iron Curtain. But I can assure you that, when I get too involved or worried in the intricacies of this problem and their possible conflict with the personal one that may build up in the U.S., I always remind myself of the fine old proverb "Always take your job seriously, never yourself." So, no matter what happens, I hope I am still safe from becoming completely self-centered and impossibly egotistical by remembering this favorite saying of old [Gen.] Fox Conner.

I cannot tell you how delighted I am to know that you are a member of the Central Committee for selecting recipients of important scholarships. I am certain you will like the work; the longer you stay with it the more rewarding you will feel it.

Please don't take too seriously your own resolution not to talk to me again about Navy personalities. I assure you there are only a few of them I know well. I think that I have met [Adm.] Lynde [D.] McCormick. He is soon coming through here for a visit. I have heard a lot of fine things about him.

Incidentally, I have tried hard to put across to America's leading military figures, as well as to those of important allied countries, what is really involved in the establishment of a large Allied Command. The first point is that when nations find it necessary to establish military commands that are as high in the hierarchy of control as is a Supreme command, we enter the zone of combined political, military and strategic decision. It matters little from what special arm or service the commander may come. The problems pertaining to a true Supreme command are partially military, but they are also partially psychological, industrial, financial and political. (Politics in the sense of relationships among the nations.) The need is for an individual who will take all these varying and variable considerations and get from them a reasonable answer out of which he can formulate broad military decisions to issue to subordinates who are, themselves, normally, combined or joint commanders. The search should therefore be for the individual. Instead, we normally decide on what nation and service should assume responsibility of command and then, having limited ourselves in choice, we try to select the individual deemed best suited for the task.

Actually, the title "Supreme" was manufactured in World War II. It was to apply to commanders who had responsibilities extending over a goodly and important section of the earth's surface. It was to apply only in the event that he commanded troops of more than one nation and, on top of this, important contingents from more than one of the three services. For this kind of job, there is no reason whatsoever that a suitably qualified admiral could not command at SHAPE or at any other similar setup. (I admit that this observation would not apply to the Atlantic Command because it is mostly naval. I see very little reason for that commander to worry too much about forces other than naval with some supporting air. He will certainly be not deeply plunged into the political, economic, industrial and psychological problems of Europe and the North Atlantic countries.)

However, you can see from all this that our ancient ideas of military organization and training (I am speaking now only of the very highest echelons) must be revised, enlarged and expanded to meet the needs of this modern day. It is necessary to select young men and begin training them on the broadest possible basis. I am convinced that all of us attach too much importance to routine military command in time of peace. We cling to the naive belief that local tactical command constitutes the true basis of the service man's development. Not only is that the easiest part, but the broad education of our most gifted men will not permit the luxury of too much emphasis on "professional" chores. We will return him often enough to troops to retain the touch and feel of command—then get him on to the hard work!

Well, I see that I have here opened up such a broad subject that I must wait until you and I can have an evening to ourselves, and over our coffee, try to agree that the world has difficulty keeping up to the vision, the wisdom, and the experienced advice that we jointly are constantly ready to offer it. I had a fortunate break and a light schedule this morning, but I have now used up my time. Give my love to Ibby and, of course, always the best to yourself.

As ever,

The campaign for the nomination, which Eisenhower won only after a bitter struggle with Robert Taft and the party's conservatives, and the subsequent campaign for the presidency, which he won in a landslide over Illinois' Governor Adlai E. Stevenson, left little time for personal correspondence; and the letters from this period are hurried and brief. One of the few substantive issues that Eisenhower discussed in them involved the so-called tidelands oil controversy. At issue was whether the states or the federal government would control oil-rich lands submerged between the low-water mark and the three-mile limit or other historic states' boundaries. The Supreme Court had ruled that these submerged lands belonged to the United States government. Eisenhower, however, whose supporters included a number of prominent oilmen, took the states' (and industry's) position. In 1953 he would sign legislation reversing the Court's decision and turning over these lands to the states.

101

12 July 1952

Dear Swede:

You will have to forgive me if I put off the answering of your fine letter to some future date. I read yours last evening, and I would certainly like to have the time right now to discuss some of the questions you raise. I shall mention only two.

With respect to the waters adjacent to our coast line, did you ever read the official resolutions and documents by which Texas entered the Union? My opinion as to where title rested was based solely upon what looked to me like a definite contract which gave Texas possession up to three leagues from their coast line.

Since I first made this statement, the Supreme Court has ruled otherwise—but it is still difficult for me to understand exactly how they reached their decision. Quite naturally if this were correct in the case of Texas, I do not see how we could discriminate against other states.

One other thing on this particular point. Did you ever compare the record of conservation of Texas oil, under state law, with the record of the federal government in such places as Teapot Dome? Actually, of course, I am not any fervent disciple on either side of the question. My position—if you can call it that—is based solely on what I thought was the sanctity of a contract. Beyond that I have not attempted to reason it out exhaustively.

You think that an eighteen year-old should not vote. I am going to send to you with this letter a guest editorial that appeared recently in the Denver *Post*. It was written by a nineteen year old girl, and I should like for you to decide whether you think she is capable of voting. It is possible that some states have intelligence tests for voters. I am not familiar with the law in each of the forty-eight. However, I would venture that the girl who wrote this little editorial and, indeed, any high school graduate, can pass any intelligence test that is set up in any state. When you add to this the fact that it is my humble opinion that eighteen year olds today know as much as we did at twenty-five, you get some inkling of what I am getting at. The radio, television, increased numbers of publications of all kinds, and a greater variety of schooling available to the young, have all served to bring them along faster than we developed in our time. Of course the federal government has nothing to do with this question at all. It is a matter for each state to decide for itself. Fighting and voting may be two different things, but I still feel that if a man is called upon to help defend his country on the battlefield, he ought to have some little voice in helping to determine its policies.

Love to Ibby, and as always, warm regards to you.

Sincerely,

In his letter of August 8, Swede had enclosed a letter from Professor George C. Taylor, a Shakespearean scholar at the University of South Carolina. Taylor reported widespread support for Eisenhower among leading Democrats such as South Carolina's Governor James F. Byrnes. But he also warned that if Eisenhower were to come out for civil rights, then "all our plans will fall flat." Eisenhower didn't need the advice. Indeed, he had earlier written to his friend Lucius Clay that he did not consider "race relations" to be an issue.

---

14 August 1952

Dear Swede:

It is good of you to send me Dr. Taylor's letters. They confirm many of the reports from the South I have been getting. As you know, we are devoting particular attention to the southern front in our planning just now, and I believe we will work out the problem satisfactorily. Reports like yours are a big help.

I hope you are having some pleasant weather in your delightful Chapel Hill.

Sincerely,

By the time this brief note was written, the campaign was in its final month. Although Eisenhower and his advisors remained supremely confident, no one, with the memory of Truman's upset victory in 1948 still fresh, was predicting a sure thing. As Swede wrote, "I wouldn't say I think it's 'in the bag.' I don't!"

16 October 1952

Dear Swede:

Thank you for taking the time to write me your thoughtful letter of October 8th. I appreciate it very much—not only as an expression of your faith and confidence, but also as a more objective evaluation of the situation which tends to be confusing when one is in the very center of it.

During the past few weeks, I have been confronted with a number of very difficult decisions. I have always been guided by what, in my opinion, would be best for the nation as a whole rather than what might appear to be the most popular thing to do under any given set of circumstances. I am convinced that leadership in the political as well as in other spheres consists largely in making progress through compromise—but that does not mean compromise with basic principles.

It is reassuring to know that, in the last analysis, you have concurred with my line of reasoning.

Mamie joins me in love to Ibby and yourself—and we hope that we can find time for a visit after the pressures of this campaign are over.

Sincerely,

On November 4, Eisenhower won in a landslide. In early December he left for Korea to keep a promise that he had made during the closing days of the campaign. In his letter of November 27, Swede drew Eisenhower's attention to an "anti-Mamie" editorial by North Carolina newspaperman and Truman's biographer Jonathan W. Daniels.

8 December 1952

Dear Swede:

A thousand thanks for your highly interesting letter. I wish I could answer it as you deserve.

It happens that this note is being written aboard the U.S.S. *Helena* about five hours out of Wake on the way to Hawaii. At the former island a group of cabinet officer designates and a few other trusted advisors boarded the ship. Within a few minutes conferences started and for the next three days I shall be busy indeed.

For quite a while my opinion of Jonathan Daniels has been of very low order. Your letter with its information that he undertook to write an anti-Mamie editorial simply eliminates him from my mind as anyone worth thinking about.

I am glad you converted your little friend Charlie [a young Stevenson supporter]—I hate to see youngsters hurt or bitterly disappointed. Tell him that I hope that I shall see him some day so that I can thank him in person for accepting me.

With respect to military aides I have decided that they shall be in the grade of lieutenant colonel and commanders. I do not want military advisors in the White House; that is the job for the Chiefs of Staff. Not long ago someone told me that each of the present three aides has three assistants. It is the case of the old story, "Big fleas have little fleas ad infinitum."

Give my love to Ibby and take care of yourself,

Sincerely,

P.S. I expect you to carry out your promise to write even though you don't hear from me.

1953

Swede and his daughter Alice attended Eisenhower's inauguration in January 1953, were seated "about 100 feet on your port
bow," but had no chance to speak to him. Eisenhower's letters to
Swede during the busy spring of 1953 were short and routine
which—together with the fact that they were signed "DE" instead
of "Ike"—revived Swede's insecurities. "Perhaps . . . I've been a
bit too brash in my communications," he wrote on July 15.
Eisenhower replied in the long, reassuring letter that follows. In it
he attempts to outline his ideas on presidential leadership and to
explain his response to the demagogic Wisconsin Senator Joseph
R. McCarthy, whom Swede and others had been urging Eisenhower to "crack down on."

21 July 1953

Dear Swede:
    The arrival of your letter reminded me that it has been far too
long since I heard from you. My natural impulse would be to do a
little complaining at this point—but when I found, at the end of
your letter, that you are in the business of marrying off your
youngest daughter, I automatically forgave all sins of omission.

Eisenhower's first inaugural, 20 January 1953 (National Park Service photograph, courtesy of Dwight D. Eisenhower Library). Chief Justice Fred M. Vinson administers the oath of office as Harry S. Truman, Herbert Hoover, and Richard M. Nixon look on.

As to the "DE" instead of "Ike," I found to my amazement—once I was actually sitting behind this desk—that I became somewhat of an embarrassment to many of my old friends. They didn't want to call me openly—or at least in front of others—by my nickname, and this embarrassment apparently carried over in some cases into their letters. They used all kinds of dodges to avoid extremes of informality and formality, and I soon found that it seemed better to fall in, at least partially, with their own ideas than it was to engage in a long and fruitless argument. One or two of my former correspondents have even cut me off their list—I think for no other reason in the world than that they felt somewhat embarrassed in addressing me by a formal title and yet they could not quite practice the informality that once characterized their friendships.

This is, of course, only one of the many personal problems that come to a man in this particular position. In your own case, it was nothing but habit that made me use the "DE" because, certainly, no question of embarrassment or strain had ever showed up between us—thank the Lord! After this, when you receive a communication from me, look first at the signature. If I have made an error, you send it back *without* reading it, and I will get back on the rails.

This business of making decisions for America brings me strange experiences. I recall almost daily an observation attributed to Napoleon that went something like this: "The genius in war is a man that can do the *average* thing when everybody else is growing hysterical or panicky in the excitement of the moment." Of course you know that I have always striven to prepare myself as much as possible for the known or calculable requirements of any job assigned me. In this particular post such intentions and practices have to be almost completely discarded. This is because of the infinite variety of problems presented, and the rapidity with which they are placed in front of the responsible individual for action. Consequently, the struggle is to apply common sense—to reach an average solution.

The one thing that must never be forgotten is that when outsiders come in, always they have an axe to grind. If a man comes in protesting bitterly against any increase in second class mail rates, it is not because he has a burning desire to serve the best interests of the public; it is because he has a burning desire to save the amount it would take out of his pocketbook. Even within government itself, these distorted and selfish views are encountered. For example, you are, of course, personally acquainted with some of the inter-service difficulties resulting from granite-like support of a special or parochial viewpoint. These same quarrels I find endlessly in every department of government.

Fortunately these instances and practices are offset by the numbers of people in governmental service who are completely dedicated individuals. I do not mean merely the persons of cabinet rank, selected, of course, by the President. It extends on down through the services, both on the appointive and on the career side. All of these individuals are the ones that help the Head in reaching a common sense, average solution. They are alert for the phony argument and the selfish motive and the untrustworthy individual. They help to meet the deficiencies of a faulty memory, a deteriorating disposition, and any tendency toward the pessimistic or the morbid.

The point of this recitation is that even the matter of reaching a common sense solution—or making an average decision—is not one that can be performed by an individual operating alone.

I was interested in a statement of yours in which you express your satisfaction that "at last you are ready to crack down on McCarthy." Now I have no doubt that you are correct in the later statement in the same paragraph where you say, "I have always known that you feel about him much as I do." At the same time, I must say that I am not quite certain as to the meaning of your first expression. Again referring to the special significance or, let us say, the popular standing of the Presidency, it is quite clear that whenever the President takes part in a newspaper trial of some individual of whom he disapproves, one thing is automatically accomplished. This is an increase in the headline value of the individual attacked.

I think that the average honorable individual cannot understand to what lengths certain politicians would go for publicity. They have learned a simple truth in American life. This is that the most vicious kind of attack from one element always creates a very great popularity, amounting to almost hero worship, in an opposite fringe of society. Because of this, as you well know, Huey Long had his idolaters. Every attack on him increased their number (an expression of the under-dog complex) and enhanced the fervor of his avowed supporters.

When you have a situation like this, you have an ideal one for the newspapers, the television and the radio, to exploit, to exaggerate and to perpetuate. In such a situation I disagree completely with the "crack down" theory. I believe in the positive approach. I believe that we should earnestly support the practice of American principles in trials and investigations—we should teach and preach decency and justice. We should support—even militantly support—people whom we know to be unjustly attacked, whether they are public servants or private citizens. In this case, of course, it is necessary to be certain of facts if the defense is to be a personal one. Of course, the indirect defense accomplished through condemnation of unfair methods is always applicable.

Persistence in these unspectacular but sound methods will, in my opinion, produce results that may not be headlines, but they will be permanent because they will earn the respect of fair-minded citizens—which means the vast bulk of our population. To give way in anger or irritation to an outburst intended to excoriate some individual, his motives and his methods, could do far more to destroy the position and authority of the attacker than it would do to damage the attacked.

Of course, it is really useless to tell you all these things. You are well aware of them. But it is always easy to grow verbose when I write to you.

The part of your letter that talked about some of the "pap" being written about me gave me quite a smile for the simple reason that I rarely, if ever, read any of these things. Once in a while I see an editorial dealing with the work I am now doing and the manner of its performance. This I try to read and apply objectively, but the old stories of smoking corn silk and fishing for mudcat are written for someone else, not for me.

I agree with you as to the convenience represented in the *Williamsburg* [the presidential yacht, a favorite of Roosevelt and Truman, the use of which Eisenhower had decided to forgo]. We liked her. But I am committed to an Administration of economy, bordering on or approaching austerity. So in spite of the fact that I felt she performed a desirable, if not almost an essential service, I felt that the very word "yacht" created a symbol of luxury in the public mind that would tend to defeat some of the purposes I was trying to accomplish. For the same reason I gave up the Presidential quarters at Key West. I have kept only the little camp up in the Catoctins. It has been renamed "Camp David." "Shangri-La" was just a little fancy for a Kansas farm boy.

Give my love to Ibby, and, of course, all the best to yourself.

As ever,

At the Bermuda "summit" conference, Eisenhower had pressed the French both for a more vigorous prosecution of the war in Indochina (which the United States was to a large degree financing through its foreign- and military-aid programs) and for the ratification of the European Defense Community (EDC). His efforts were unsuccessful in both instances. On his return, he delivered a much-heralded speech at the United Nations on the "Peaceful Atom," urging that the United States and the Soviet

Union join in contributing fissionable materials to an international "bank" from which other nations could draw for nonmilitary purposes—"agriculture, medicine, and [the production of] abundant electrical energy in the power starved areas of the world."

His hopes for the Republican legislative program were soon to be dashed by the bitter controversies inspired by Joe McCarthy, which would dominate American politics throughout much of 1954. And he would soon change his opinions about a number of those whom he had considered to be his possible successors. Swede, meanwhile, had suffered another heart attack, had been bedridden for six weeks, and remained, as he put it, "out of circulation to a great extent."

---

24 December 1953

Personal and Confidential

Dear Swede:

Your most recent letter to me was written on November twenty-sixth, more than a week before I went to Bermuda. The period has been one of the busiest of my life; but, though at times I have felt almost at the point of exhaustion, there have still been moments of real satisfaction that have made all the rest of it seem worthwhile.

I shall not attempt to give you a personal diary covering the past three weeks. I cannot set down in chronological order all of the ideas, actions and impulses that have been part of the innumerable conferences, meetings and discussions that have, at times, seemed to be never ending. But introductions and alibis will get me no further along. So without further ado, I shall try to give you a decently coherent account of the things that come immediately to memory.

First in order would be the Bermuda meeting. With respect to that trip, my initial observation is that it provides a good example of how useless it is to tell the full truth to the press—at least when the representatives of that estate want to believe otherwise. On

The December 1953 meeting in Bermuda with French Premier Joseph Laniel and British Prime Minister Winston Churchill (courtesy of Dwight D. Eisenhower Library).

two occasions I informed the individuals at White House press conferences that there was no purpose of the Bermuda meeting that could be defined in terms of agreements sought or arrangements to be definitely fixed. I told them that the purpose was purely that of meeting in an informal way with friends in order that we could discuss together our common interests in various portions of the globe and compare our approaches to the problems that confront us daily. I warned that there would be no agenda—an error of omission was that I failed to say there would be no "final communique."

As a result of that failure, all other officials at the conference, influenced by routine and custom, and needled by some two hundred press, radio, television and newsreel representatives, spent a great deal of time on the exact wording of a final, "combined" statement. It bored me immeasurably and struck me as typifying futility. When people get to arguing heatedly over such details, I inevitably recall the old saying "picking nits with boxing gloves."

In spite of this frustrating item, the meeting as a whole was productive, especially in providing opportunity for necessary conversations with the British. This was not as true in the case of the French because of the known certainty that this particular French government would not be of long life.

At times Winston [Churchill] seemed to be his old and hearty self, full of vim and determination. At others he seemed almost to wander in his mind. I must confess that occasionally I suspected this latter was almost a deliberately adopted mannerism rather than an involuntary habit. At least it seemed to come over him only when the subject under discussion or the argument presented was distasteful to him.

The French situation, currently symbolized by their almost futile effort to elect a President, was clearly felt also at Bermuda. The answers were always "Yes, but" or "No, unless."

Actually, France's situation is merely symptomatic of what is happening to the entire world. There is the extreme Right. In France these people are the deGaullists, while in the world scene they are Fascist dictatorships, largely found now in Spanish-speaking or in the Arab countries.

There is the extreme Left, in France and in the world, Communistic.

In between these two extremes is a vast center group which in basic beliefs has much in common, and, for this reason, should be a closely knit organization. In point of fact this vast center or "middle of the Road" group prefers to shut its eyes to the dangers represented in the extremes—in the current state of affairs, the only threatening extreme is Communism. The group of nations of which this center is constituted constantly indulge in all kinds of divisive arguments and name-calling that grow so important in their cumulative effect as to nullify any attempt toward unity in working against the common enemy.

So—just as the French cannot agree upon firm policies respecting the prosecution of the Indo-China war nor decide what they want to do with respect to EDC, we find that the world cannot agree on basic policies concerning trade with the Communists, firming up cooperative plans that would permit us all to advance economically and politically, nor even decide how we can best protect ourselves along the sensitive European front.

India would rather see Pakistan weak and helpless in front of a Russian threat than to see that country grow strong enough to give substance to its hope of annexing Kashmir. France would rather see Germany weak and helpless in Europe than to see that country strong enough to serve as an effective bar against possible Russian invasion. In the latter event, France is fearful that German strength might again be used against her. Of course to us this particular fear seems senseless, in view of our guarantees that no country admitted into the combined European defensive system would be allowed to attack another.

There is no use belaboring the point nor pursuing the analogy too far. The fact is, however, that while we get almost disgusted with the picture that France currently presents, we need only to look at the rest of the world—indeed to ourselves—to see many points of similarity.

I think I have digressed sufficiently far from Bermuda that I should come back there just long enough to say that I left the Islands one morning, flew to New York, and that afternoon made a talk to the UN.

That particular talk had been evolving in our minds and plans for many weeks. Quite a while ago I began to search around for any kind of an idea that could bring the world to look at the atomic problem in a broad and intelligent way and still escape the impasse to action created by Russian intransigence in the matter of mutual or neutral inspection of resources. I wanted, additionally, to give our people and the world some faint idea of the size of the distance already travelled by this new science—but to do it in such a way as not to create new alarm.

One day I hit upon the idea of actual physical donations by Russia and the United States—with Britain also in the picture in a minor way—and to develop this thought in such a way as to provide at the very least a calm and reasonable atmosphere in which the whole matter could again be jointly studied. Once the decision was taken to propose such a plan in some form, the whole problem became one of treatment, choice of time, place and circumstance, and the niceties of language. I had, of course, a lot of excellent help—but I personally put on the text a tremendous amount of time.

Throughout the friendly world reactions have been good; our official messages have been much like the public statements you have seen in the press. The Soviets have now, at last, moved toward a meeting, though not without their customary grumbling, griping, and some sneering. We will see now what the next step brings forth! But all in all I believe that the effort up to this point has been well worth while, and has done something to create a somewhat better atmosphere both at home and abroad.

A week after finishing the UN talk, my Cabinet and I had to be ready to meet the Republican legislative leaders and go over with them the legislative program we had prepared during these past months. We knew exactly where we wanted to go in the matter of principle and we were quite sure of the basic direction that we would take in each of the several important fields that together would make up an entire program. But it was very necessary to get together with the legislative leaders for several purposes:

(a). To gather from the legislative leaders their impressions of the sentiment of the country, compare their reactions with ours, and thus arrive at an order of precedence or priority in the presentation of the program.

(b). Under the principles and purposes laid out by the Administration, to work out applicable legislative methods, as well as modifying small details to add to the attractiveness or popularity of the particular program.

(c). To renew the habit of cooperative effort between the Executive and Legislative Departments.

(d). To bring out that the Republican Party, headed by the President, had reached that point where a *combined, concerted effort to put over a progressive, enlightened legislative program was mandatory!*

It is, of course, necessary for all to understand that success will lead to continuing governmental responsibility. Failure would lead to an adverse result which would be exactly what was deserved in the circumstances. Since the President, under our system, must take the lead in the presentation of such programs, the simple truth is that the mass of Republican and independent supporters have got to be behind the Administration—or else.

The meetings were on the whole successful—so far as we can determine—far beyond our expectations. Of course only the stress of actual Congressional debate and voting will tell the final story, but I am hopeful.

I do not mean by any of the above that mere partisan Republican support is, under the existing circumstances in Congress, sufficient to the success of a legislative program. We have got to have the support of reasonable and enlightened Democrats and I shall certainly do all I can to deserve that support and to act,

116

personally, in such a way as to encourage the Democrats to give it to us.

When last Saturday night arrived and the three days of conferences, luncheon meetings and arguments had become history, I was so weary and tired that I doubt that I could have spoken pleasantly to my best friend. However, I did have the distinct feeling that we could look forward to truly intelligent and cooperative work in both Executive and Legislative branches during the next session of the Congress. If that comes about, I will, a few months later, be reaching the halfway mark in my political career with some sense of real accomplishment, to say nothing of legitimate reason to hope that improvement and progress will characterize our country and the world during the approximate future.

I started this letter in the hope and the belief that it would really be informative. I have just glanced through what I finished yesterday and find that it is almost a dud, especially for one who makes a habit of reading the daily papers. In an effort to include a piece of news—but after all it will not be news to you—I shall tell you what would be classed as "Secret Intentions." It involves 1956, and January 20, 1957. With respect to the political campaign of '56, my position will be exactly as I determined it would be when finally I gave way in '52 to the convictions and arguments of some of my friends. I shall never again be a candidate for anything, and I so told my friends two years ago. This determination is a fixed decision (subject to modification *only* in the case of some worldwide cataclysm that I cannot now foresee and which would make political change at such a moment almost catastrophic for our country). Of course I realize that American politics demands that a President keep his intentions secret in this regard; otherwise, it is assumed his whole influence on the political scene would disappear and he could not possibly lead in the development of a legislative program. So, for the moment, I shall observe this so-called political axiom, but this will certainly in no way affect my intentions!

Meanwhile, I am doing my part to make certain that the policies in which I firmly believe will have younger and abler champions when I step off the stage. As I have more than once told you, the man who, from the standpoint of knowledge of human and governmental affairs, persuasiveness in speech and dedication to our country, would make the best President I can think of is my young brother, Milton. Under no circumstances would I ever say this publicly because, in the first place, I do not think he is physically strong enough to take the beating. In the second place, any effort to make him the candidate in 1956 would properly be resented by our people. So he is out so far as I am concerned. Anyway, I am certain that such a thought has never crossed his mind and, if it ever did, he would reach the same obvious conclusion that I have just stated.

But here are some names of people that I am constantly trying to keep in the public eye so as to let the American people know more and more about them. Each is able, clean and energetic, and also important, relatively young. Each is a good executive—and would certainly have my support—if, at that time, my support would be helpful. [UN Ambassador Henry Cabot] Lodge, [Vice-President Richard M.] Nixon, [Attorney General Herbert] Brownell [Jr.], [Mutual Security Administrator Harold E.] Stassen, [Deputy Attorney General William P.] Rogers, [Secretary of the Army Robert] Stevens, and one or two others in the Executive Department. In Congress, [Indiana Congressman] Charlie [A.] Halleck is a standout, and along with him there are a number of young men developing who could easily become headliners before 1956. They include [Senator Charles E.] Potter, [Senator Barry M.] Goldwater, possibly [Senator William F.] Knowland and others.

All I am saying here is that, far from trying to keep young men out of the spotlight, it is my hope to push them into it and so have ready a group of young men who are not only able but who will have the publicity value that a political party always seeks in its candidate.

Of course I have no fear that you will ever reveal this information to anyone—but I want you personally to have it so that if a time ever comes when you see me even *appearing* to waver from strict adherence to this pledge—you are to take drastic steps to see that I do not become more of a damned fool than I was in '52.

Merry Christmas and Happy New Year to Ibby and your nice family.

As ever,

1954

In early January, Eisenhower sent Swede a reproduction of one of his paintings. He wrote again, two weeks later, but only to bemoan the fact that he had so little time to write. By mid March, when he finally wrote at greater length, he was preoccupied with, among other things, his legislative program, a mild recession, the attempt by Ohio Republican John W. Bricker to win passage of an amendment to the Constitution limiting the president's power to make treaties, the French struggle against the Vietminh in Indochina, and the growing controversy between Joe McCarthy and the Army.

7 January 1954

Dear Swede:

Originally I had no thought of inflicting on my good friends the print that you will find coming to you in the mail. It is a reproduction of what I, with some embarrassment, call a "portrait" of Lincoln. The real reason that I am sending it is because I find myself surrounded only by people who are trying to keep my spirits at an all-time high and who, out of all reason, praise the amateurish effort of which you will now have a copy.

At the very least it brings to you my best wishes for a wonderful year in 1954.

As ever,

26 January 1954

Dear Swede:

The days go by at their accustomed pace, leaving little time for the more pleasurable pursuits of life such as indulging in correspondence with good friends. Even now I can do little more than to tell you again how much I enjoy your letters, and to urge you to write whenever you feel the impulse to do so.

Occasionally I run into old friends of yours who tell me they have been to Chapel Hill for a visit. Each time this occurs I make up my mind to send you a letter telling of the circumstances under which I encountered your friends.

As you now know from the total failure of such reports to reach you, my memory plays me tricks—and by the time I get to the office I am in the midst of politics, economics, education, foreign trade, and cotton and tobacco surpluses.

All of which is merely preliminary to asking that you give my love to Ibby, and of course, my warm regard to yourself.

As ever,

18 March 1954

Dear Swede:

I suddenly realize that too much time had elapsed since I last wrote you an intimate report on the "State of the Union." I believe I did manage to congratulate you on your (non-existent, but nevertheless numerical) birthday, but it has been months otherwise.

The interval since the opening of this session of Congress has been turbulent, as reported too fully in the papers. The press has harped, or so it seems from this nerve center, on certain demagogic individuals and practices, and exaggerated, out of all proportion in my opinion, their importance to the nation as a whole. These things, I am convinced, will run their inevitable course—and I refuse to deviate from my declared position, in spite of the urgings of some of my most valued friends and associates in government.

Three things have of this day occupied my time and attention. (I say three, excluding, of course, the inevitable handshaking or button-pushing ceremonies that seem daily and inevitably to intrude on the business of government.)

One of these problems is the recent declaration by the Secretary of Agriculture [Ezra Taft Benson] that as of April first supports for dairy products will be reduced from 90% of parity to 75%. This announcement is in accordance with common sense. It has, however, been widely interpreted as a violation of the principle of gradualism that we have advocated in flexible price supports. This may put us in a hole in establishing our sincerity when we talk of gradualism as a feature of the farm policy. In addition, there is no question that it will somewhat diminish the purchasing power of the people in the dairy producing states, and inevitably add to our burdens there. I personally think the Secretary of Agriculture made a mistake in failing to take smaller bites—though I hasten to add that he did so with my general approval and on his understanding of the law, believing it to be compulsory. The error, if *any*, was merely in failing to search for some means of acting a bit more gradually, even though we have butter, milk, cheese and all other dairy products flooding the country. In saying this I want to stress, too, that there is no man in government more dedicated and devoted, and more selfless and sincere, than is Ezra Benson.

Another problem of the day and of the past weeks (now successfully concluded as I dictate this around five o'clock) has been the struggle in the House over the Administration's tax program. You know as well as I the attack the program has been under, and there is no need here to repeat the views I expressed in my television talk on Monday night. But I do want to say that I am firmly convinced that, under existing circumstances, the Administration's bill is a well thought out program of tax reduction and economic stimulation. It is designed to do the greatest good for the greatest number of our citizens, under domestic and world conditions of this moment. The fact that the bill was successfully pushed through the House was due to the great work done by Charlie Halleck, Joe Martin [Speaker of the House] and a couple of others up on the Hill. On this particular issue I found the Administration had the good solid team work in the House that it should have had and did not have in certain other matters in the Senate, notably the "Bricker Amendment."

The third major problem of the day is the increasingly bad situation in Indo-China. As you know, the Vietminh continue their assault on Dien Bien Phu, and the situation there becomes increasingly disturbing. I hope the French will have the stamina to stick it out; because a defeat in that area will inevitably have a serious psychological effect on the French. I suspect that this particular attack was launched by the Communists to gain an advantage to be used at the Geneva Conference. At any rate, it is just another of the problems that is dumped in my lap—in this particular case, of course, there is little I can do except to wait it out and hope for the best.

You must forgive my rambling—but I do find some release from the tensions of the day in writing in this fashion. It provides the next best thing to seeing you.

My love to Ibby, and of course, as always, the very best to yourself,

As ever,

_____

The war in Vietnam between the French and the Communist-led Vietminh had been going on for eight years and was now nearing its climax in a battle over the isolated French stronghold at Dien Bien Phu. The French, though Eisenhower does not mention it here, were appealing for United States intervention and had received strong support both from Secretary of State John Foster Dulles and from Vice-President Nixon. Eisenhower himself told a press conference that Indochina was like a "falling domino" whose collapse would threaten the entire Pacific basin; Nixon would tell a meeting of newspaper editors that "we must take the risk now by putting American boys in"; and the head of the Joint Chiefs of Staff, Adm. Arthur W. Radford, would put the final touches on *Operation Vulture*, a proposed American airstrike at

Dien Bien Phu. The French, however, were not willing to meet Eisenhower's conditions—a clear-cut commitment to independence for the Vietnamese, the "internationalization" of the war, and, implicit in this, a determinative role for the United States in its conduct.

The defeat of the French and the subsequent Geneva settlements provided a framework for peace in Indochina, though on terms that almost everyone recognized would quickly lead to Vietminh control of all of Vietnam. In its efforts to avoid this outcome, the Eisenhower administration would subvert the Geneva agreements and lay the groundwork for the expanded United States commitment that would occur under President's Kennedy and Johnson.

By April the army-McCarthy hearings were playing to a packed audience in the old Senate caucus room and to a national television audience of millions. The army, which had been harassed by McCarthy throughout 1953, had accused the senator of using his office to seek special favors for G. David Schine, a young staff member who had been drafted. McCarthy counterattacked by accusing the army of holding Schine as a "hostage." The investigation of these charges and countercharges was conducted by the Senate's Subcommittee on Permanent Investigations, McCarthy's own committee, from which the senator had reluctantly stepped down.

Eisenhower was dismayed by the proceedings. As he suggests in this letter, quite typically, he would have much preferred a decorous and orderly investigation by an administrative agency such as the army's inspector general. He nevertheless stuck by his decision not to engage the senator publicly, though he was widely criticized for doing so. Eisenhower did move against McCarthy indirectly and through intermediaries. It would remain for the Senate itself to discipline McCarthy, however, which it did in late 1954 when it voted to censure him.

27 April 1954

Dear Swede:

A few nights ago I made a talk before the American Newspaper Publishers' Association. In the course of the talk I urged the need for better understanding in America of today's domestic and world problems; I likewise urged the need for a greater two-way flow of information between us and nations abroad. I tried to point out that regardless of other means of developing understandings and providing information the most effective vehicle was still the publicity media of the several nations. The consequence of this kind of thinking is that newspapers have a very definite responsibility to our country to inform it accurately and adequately, and that while we must sustain the rights of a free press, it seems clear that the free press must try to promote reader-understanding as well as to cater to reader-interest.

To this talk I have had no adverse reaction from outsiders or laymen; but I have received a number of criticisms from publishers themselves. The central theme of the criticism has been "Why should *he* attempt to tell us about our business?" Personally I thought I was rather mild in expressing my feelings in the matter, but where I have made any attempt to reply to the friendly publishers who have shared this critical view, I have said only two things—first, "Are you operating a grocery store for immediate profit or do you regard the publishing of a newspaper as partaking of a public service? If the latter is the case, then you certainly assume responsibilities the discharge of which are of great interest to governmental officials."

My second observation has been, "When have you hesitated to tell me how to run my business? Admittedly I am a public servant and therefore subject, in all my public actions, to criticism. But, again, assuming that you do admit that the publishing of a newspaper should be as much a public service as a 'commercial venture' you are also to that degree a public servant and I have a right to criticize you."

Beyond this, I did not, of course, make any sweeping allegations against the American press. Consequently any hurt feelings must be because someone felt that the shoe fit—but uncomfortably.

In my last letter I remember that I mentioned Dien Bien Phu. It still holds out and while the situation looked particularly desperate during the past week, there now appears to be a slight improvement and the place may hold on for another week or ten days. The general situation in Southeast Asia, which is rather dramatically epitomized by the Dien Bien Phu battle, is a complicated one that has been a long time developing. It involves many talks on the international level and the frantic desire of the French to remain a world power, but at the same time defeating themselves through their deep divisions and consequent indecisiveness at home.

For more than three years I have been urging upon successive French governments the advisability of finding some way of "internationalizing" the war; such action would be proof to all the world and particularly to the Viet Namese that France's purpose is not colonial in character but is to defeat Communism in the region and to give the natives their freedom. The reply has always been vague, containing references to national prestige, Constitutional limitations, inevitable effects upon the Moroccan and Tunisian peoples, and dissertations on plain political difficulties and battles within the French Parliament. The result has been that the French have failed entirely to produce any enthusiasm on the part of the Vietnamese for participation in the war. (Incidentally, did you ever stop to think that if the British had, in our War of the Revolution, treated as equals the Americans who favored them—whom they called Loyalists and we called Tories—the job of Washington would have been much more difficult, if not impossible. I have read that when the entire colonial forces in the field numbered not more than twenty-five thousand, that there were fifty thousand Americans serving in some capacity with and for the British. Yet no really effective service was rendered by these people because the British persisted in treating them as "colonials and inferiors.")

In any event, any nation that intervenes in a civil war can scarcely expect to win unless the side in whose favor it intervenes possesses a high morale based upon a war purpose or cause in which it believes. The French have used weasel words in promising independence and through this one reason as much as anything else, have suffered reverses that have been really inexcusable.

The British are frightened, I *think*, by two things. First, they have a morbid obsession that any positive move on the part of the free world may bring upon us World War III. Secondly, they are desperately concerned about the safety of Hong Kong. For the moment the Chinese Communists are not molesting Hong Kong and the British are fearful that if they should be identified as opponents of the Communists in the Indo-China affair, they might suffer the loss of Hong Kong at any moment. All this is conjecture, but in respect to this particular point, my own view is in almost direct opposition. I personally feel that if the Communists would take a good smacking in Indo-China, they would be more likely to leave Hong Kong severely alone for a long time. Moreover, if a "concert of nations" should undertake to protect Western interests in this critical section of the globe, it would appear that Hong Kong would almost automatically fall within the protected zone.

Just what the outcome will be, of course, is still largely a guess, but in any event I feel that the situation is a shade—but only a shade—brighter than it was a week or so ago.

The McCarthy-Army argument, and its reporting, are close to disgusting. It saddens me that I must feel ashamed for the United States Senate. Other than that, I doubt that I have any opinions on the subject that are greatly different from your own, so I will pass it up for the moment.

One of the features of service life that I miss in this job is an "Inspector General's" service. Visitors here—usually meaning to be helpful—are quite apt to leave with me a hint that something is wrong here or wrong there, and sometimes these allegations or charges are of a grave nature.

In the Army it was so simple to turn to a properly trained and dedicated group any inspection job ranging from suspected peculation to plain incompetence, and it never occurred to me that a similar or equivalent agency would not be available in the Federal government. But there is no readily available agency to look into hints of this character. Even when they are referred to the interested departments of government, they are very likely to be handled in a rather lackadaisical manner for the simple reason that people are not accustomed to the standards of administrative accounting and responsibility that prevailed in the armed services.

* * *

I had two other subjects—but I stop here in desperation.

* * *

Love to the family.

As ever,

In regard to the development of natural resources, Eisenhower sought to replace what he called an "exclusive dependence on Federal bureaucracy" with "a partnership of state and local communities, private citizens, and the Federal Government, all working toether." In practice, this meant a much greater role for the large private utilities. He tried especially hard to arrest the growth of the popular New Deal–spawned Tennessee Valley Authority (TVA). The administration's attempt to replace a proposed TVA steam plant with one built by a private utility was abandoned, however, following revelations of conflict of interest in the celebrated Dixon-Yates controversy.

Finally, as this letter makes clear, Eisenhower also favored development, whether public or private, as opposed to the claims of conservationists. The Bureau of Reclamation's proposal to construct a large multipurpose project on the Upper Colorado River was opposed by conservationists because it authorized, among other things, the building of a dam and a reservoir within the Dinosaur National Monument. This particular provision was eventually dropped, however, before Congress completed its final action on the bill in 1956.

On a very different subject, the following letter reveals Eisenhower's strong commitment to the liberal trading policies of the Roosevelt and Truman administrations. He was under strong pressure from protectionists, especially in the conservative wing of his own party, to raise U.S. trade barriers. He resisted these pressures, complaining in his diary that many businessmen were "so concerned with their own particular immediate market and prosperity that they utterly fail to see that the United States cannot continue to live in a world where it must . . . export vast portions of its industrial and agricultural products unless it also imports a sufficiently great amount of foreign products to allow countries to pay for the surpluses they receive from us."

20 July 1954

Dear Swede:

For a number of years I have been serving in posts that were considered by the press as possible sources of news. Consequently, I have become used to inaccurate reporting—I think it is not too much to say that, without checking, I believe no story in a newspaper that involves thoughts, ideas or quotations. I do like to read editorials merely to find out what editors are thinking about and what they believe that America is thinking about. Here, too, I am frequently disappointed by the apparent ignorance of the facts underlying some opinion or conviction expressed by the writer.

With your last letter you enclosed an editorial having to do with the dam that is under consideration for construction in Dinosaur National Park. The statement is made that the place will be ruined for use by the public; that its scenic beauty will be forever lost.

Now I have never visited the area and so I don't want to appear to be as positive of the correctness of the views I express as was the writer of the editorial you sent. But I can't help wondering whether he bases his own opinion on a personal visit and experience or on what somebody else has said.

In any event, the records show that *last year, five hundred Americans visited the affected area.* I am not going to try to express this figure in terms of percentage of 160 million people, but if you have time to figure it out, you will not be impressed by its size. I am told that erection of the dam, with the roads leading thereto and the existence on the artificial lake of a reasonable number of suitable boats, will make the area truly accessible to travelers. It is believed that the number of visitors will jump from a figure of five hundred to many thousands, and I am further informed that the lake waters will conceal so little of what is now visible as to be unnoticeable to anyone except a crank. Possibly I am misinformed, but I venture that the reports I have are as accurate as those on which the editorialist based his opinion.

He said the principal purpose of the dam was reclamation. It is not. He even suggested that atomic power would make dams and power projects useless. Someday perhaps they will. But at this moment such a statement does not appear to me to be very potent as an argument.

As for the man who wrote the high tariff pamphlet, I hear these arguments all the time.

If it were possible to erect barriers against the trade of particular countries and to encourage trade from others, I could certainly favor some high tariffs. But this is not practicable both because of the existence of the "most favored nation clause" in our treaties and because in actual practice it would scarcely be enforceable.

Without going further afield, let us consider for just a moment the case of Mexico. We are her greatest customer; she must sell to us or her standard of living will go markedly down from even the low level at which it now exists. Already in that country there is a strong communist leaning among certain groups. Included among those individuals with such leanings is one of the most popular men in Mexico, ex President [Lázaro] Cárdenas. If we erect barriers against Mexican trade, I know that the possibility of her turning communist would mount rapidly. Our border with Mexico runs from Brownsville to the Pacific Ocean, and it is almost totally unguarded. The "wetback" problem arose out of the fact that we simply cannot provide the means to prevent Mexicans from going back and forth across the border, almost at will. If that country should turn communist, and without considering all the other evil consequences that would follow in the wake of such an event, just think of the job that we would have in closing that border tightly. The financial outlay alone would be colossal.

As of now we do not take too seriously any direct threat from Mexico. She is a weak country. But let her once form a partnership with Moscow and it takes no great imagination at all to see what would happen.

I have taken this one simple example to show that people ignore pertinent facts when they center their attention exclusively upon local matters. It is scarcely an exaggeration to say that every domestic problem of any moment must, before it can be properly solved, be examined critically against the background of our international situation. This is what so many of the after dinner speakers forget.

There are a number of things on which we should possibly have higher tariffs than we do now. But the problem may not be solved merely through consideration of local "prosperity" but on its effect upon practical cooperation among us and our international friends.

Of course I agree with the argument of the author that to throw our gates open now to "free trade" would be disastrous. But I might end this part of my letter by merely saying that anyone whose business and profits depend upon high protective tariffs is not, by any stretch of the imagination, a rugged individualist. He is just as much a kept man as is anyone who lives upon any other form of subsidy from the people of the United States.

Frankly, I think it almost idiotic to attempt any discussion of the tariff in a few paragraphs; the subject is so complex and intricate that the best that can be evolved in a short time is a few expletives, slogans and aphorisms.

When last I wrote to you, I talked something of Indo-China. That battle is now being waged as much in Geneva [where an international conference was taking place] as in the rice paddies of the Red Delta. In neither place are the French doing well. But one bright spot in the picture is that [Pierre] Mendès-France [premier of France] has turned out to be much more of a man than most people predicted. The next few days should determine what we are now up against in that area. I keep in close touch with the situation because I can imagine developments in Geneva that would make me go on the air with explanations to the people.

Congressional leaders still hope to adjourn by July 31st, but I must say that to me the prospects look very bleak. My own feeling is that I want them to go just as quickly as they will give me the *great bulk of the program recommended to them for enactment.* Already we know that there are certain items on which they won't act at this session or upon which they have acted unfavorably. But they still could make a very brilliant and fine record if they would just get going; and after all, I have to have something to fight about next session.

In the armed services I have been having a struggle with some of the civilian leadership. Whenever there comes up the subject of morale, some of my associates bring up calculations, in terms of percentages, of the disadvantages suffered by the armed services in the matter of pay. The answer they have is to "increase the armed services pay 5%." Such generalizations make me furious. For a long time I have preached such things for the armed services as:

a. Automatic increase in living allowances, based upon proper "norms."

b. Assurance to all career personnel of adequate quarters and, above all, adequate medical care for their dependents, under all circumstances.

c. Adequate survivors' benefits and pensions for dependents—whether active or retired.

d. More stable personnel policies to avoid the incessant moving around of families that now takes place because of some academic idea as to what constitutes a satisfactory "career."

When they get these things done, I am ready to examine the salary scales, but as of now I believe that, except possibly for junior officers, the salary scale is not half as important as the matters I have just mentioned.

You have probably read something in your newspapers about the struggle I am having with the fanatical supporters of TVA. The proposal I have made [to replace a proposed TVA steam plant with one built by private capital] might be challenged on the possible basis of violation of the letter of the law. But I believe that so far as logic and common sense are concerned, the proposal offers a good temporary solution to a problem that grows more difficult day by day. The facts are:

a. TVA is an existing fact, and there should be no disposition to destroy it or damage it.

b. Through TVA, supported in some part at least, by the taxes of the entire country, the Tennessee Valley area has available cheap power. Consequently, industries from other regions are showing a tendency to move into the Tennessee Valley so as to take advantage of these prices for power. Naturally, this arouses a fierce resentment on the part of competing industrialists and all the informed tax payers in other areas.

c. Because of the growing demand for power in the Tennessee region, there is now a shortage which must be supplied from somewhere.

d. The Federal Government, through the Atomic Energy Commission, is a great consumer of TVA power.

e. Consequently, the TVA fanatics assert that the Federal Government has the obligation of supplying this power.

f. Already the power potential of the streams in the region has been developed, and steam plants have been built by the Federal Government to firm up the water power of the dams already constructed. All further development must be by steam; already one-half of the power being produced is from steam plants.

With these facts at hand, the questions that arise are: "is there any limit to the number of steam plants that the Federal Government should build in the region? Should the Federal Government, having built up the system to its existing extent, now require that the locality provide for itself any additional power that it needs?"

Admittedly, it has been extremely difficult to dig out all the pertinent facts. It is for this reason that, to head TVA, I have been desperately searching for a man who is experienced in hydraulic engineering and who is completely free from any political or ideological bias of any kind. I have finally hit upon a man [Herbert D. Vogel] whose entire life has been spent in the engineering profession and who has never been connected with politics in any way. I shall send his name soon to the Senate. The only instructions I am giving him are that he is to find out the facts and report to me on an objective basis; otherwise, he is merely to run the TVA as honestly and efficiently as he knows how, and make his recommendations to the Congress and to me based upon what he believes to be the best interests of the country.

But in the meantime we have the need for power. And if the Federal Government does not build the requested steam plants (located, incidentally, way out on the periphery of the region, at West Memphis), then the Atomic Energy Commission must purchase its power from private industry or the power shortage will merely grow more aggravated.

This is what I propose.

The reason that no private individual or municipality in the area can *now* build plants and distribute power, is that all the TVA contracts contain a clause giving to the TVA a monopoly.

It seems a strange thing when, in America, there is bitterly opposed a governmental proposal that seeks no more than practical opportunity in which to take a look to see what we are doing in some of these projects that bring the Federal Government into every facet and phase of our lives.

In permitting the incessant growth of the Federal Government, we have already drifted a long way from the philosophy of Jefferson. While he was not necessarily always right, he did have sense enough to know that if Federal authority should be extended throughout the country, through various subterfuges of corporations, authorities, loans and grants, it would eventually stifle the individual freedom that our government was designed to protect and preserve.

This whole case reminds me of how much time a President has to spend in resisting pressure groups—each organized to gain for its members some advantage through Federal law or to make it possible for them to dig deep into the Federal treasury. At first blush it would not seem difficult to champion the cause of all the people against any particular segment thereof. But when you add up all the segments that have special interests in some kind of Federal preferment, the picture does not look so rosy. You might try listing them for yourself.

One of the things we need most in this country today is a general rainfall of about two inches over the entire country, and falling softly and gently over a period of about a week. If you can arrange this, you will make some of my troubles far less acute.

Give my love to Ibby and the family.

As ever,

P.S. This is really—in spite of its length—only a miniature of a day's worries—problems—etc.

D.

By the time that Eisenhower wrote this letter he was deeply involved in the election campaign, to a degree all the more surprising given his repeatedly stated aversion to political campaigning. Despite his efforts, however, the Republicans lost control of both the House and Senate, and for the the next six years, Eisenhower would be compelled to work with a Congress that was organized by the opposition party.

In the following letter, Eisenhower provides a brief rejoinder to those who were charging that he was allowing John Foster Dulles to virtually run foreign affairs. And in his discussion of Earl Warren, whom he had named to the Supreme Court in March, he reveals a stunning misapprehension of both Warren and the civil-rights issue. Eisenhower disagreed with the Court's ruling in the *Brown* vs. *Board of Education of Topeka, Kansas,* decision and would later characterize the appointment of Warren as "the biggest damfool mistake I ever made."

---

23 October 1954

Dear Swede:

Your judgment on the spinning reel coincides exactly with mine. Since 1944 when I first encountered these gadgets in France, I have been the recipient of various types of spinners—I should say one arrives about every sixty days. I leave them to those who like them. For my own fishing, I keep half a dozen fly rods ranging from about 1-½ ounces to 4-½, and I keep three favorite casting rods. I think this combination ought to see me through the fishing seasons left to me.

I skip over your comments on the election campaign. I have appeared before a number of audiences, but I strive to deal only with substantive matters—with fact and logical deduction—while staying out of political bickering.

When you mention Adlai [Stevenson], I again find myself in complete agreement with you, except that I doubt that he is a very dangerous opponent. However, if he should slip into a position of real responsibility, he would represent a great risk for the country.

As to "four-headed" foreign policy, the Democrats never succeeded in keeping people like [Nevada's Sen. Patrick] McCarran from sounding off when they so chose. So if a Republican Senator lets go once in a while, I don't know what we can do about it, even though I deplore the misunderstandings they create.

So far as Dulles is concerned, he has never made a serious pronouncement, agreement or proposal without complete and exhaustive consultation with me in advance and, of course, my approval. If your friend Senator [Samuel J.] Ervin [Dem., N.C.] would take the trouble to look up the record, he would see that Nixon belonged in the same school, although he admittedly tries to put his pronouncements into more colorful language.

You are somewhat wrong in your statement, "I know that at one time you contemplated some really drastic action in Indo-

China." What I really attempted to do was to get established in that region the conditions under which I felt the United States could properly intervene to protect its own interests. A proper political foundation for any military action was essential. Since we could not bring it about (though we prodded and argued for almost two years), I gave not even a tentative approval to any plan for massive intervention.

You are right in your conclusion that the European situation looks somewhat better. By no means have I made up my mind finally on Mendès-France. For the moment, I accept your instinctive impression as my own.

As to appointments on the Supreme Court, I think one or two observations are applicable. Your implication seems to be that Governor Warren was a "political" appointment. It was most emphatically not.

That particular vacancy occurred most unexpectedly, and the particular qualifications in the individual that should fill it were something that I studied and lived with for a number of weeks. The Chief Justice has a great many administrative tasks, as well as obvious responsibilities involving personal leadership. Along with this, he must be a statesman and, in my opinion (since I have my share of egotism), I could not do my duty unless I appointed a man whose philosophy of government was somewhat along the lines of my own. All this finally brought me down to Warren, especially as I refused to appoint anyone to the Supreme Court who was over 62 years of age. It seems to me completely futile to try to use a Supreme Court vacancy as a mere reward for long and brilliant service. If I should be succeeded by a New Deal President, a judge who is now 69 or 70 would probably create a vacancy very soon to be filled by the left-wingers. So—it seems to me that prudence demands that I secure relatively young men for any vacancies that may occur. I *wish* that I could find a number of outstanding jurists in the low 50's.

The segregation issue will, I think, become acute or tend to die out according to the character of the procedure orders that the Court will probably issue this winter. My own guess is that they will be very moderate and accord a maximum of initiative to local courts.

Give my love to the family.

As ever,

In the aftermath of the off-year elections, in which the Republicans had lost control of Congress, Eisenhower returned to the question of his candidacy in 1956 and to a general analysis of Republican politics. He makes clear here, as elsewhere, his contempt for Congress and its "demagogues," and his preference for administration over electoral politics. The letter ends with a frothy digression on "greatness."

8 December 1954

Dear Swede:

A new phase of political experience has begun for me. We have now reached the point where we have newspaper and radio argument as to whether or not I could be re-elected if I should be a 1956 candidate.

The effect on the individual (myself) of this argument is to stir up a reaction of "I will show them." Possibly, if I read the papers and listened to the radio as steadily as some others, I would be more influenced by this kind of thing. Actually I regard it as just "sound and fury" that does not raise in my own mind the slightest question as to the wisdom of my decision, long ago communicated to you.

While I don't recall the exact words of that letter [of 24 Dec. 1953], I think I did imply that the *only* thing that could possibly make me change my mind would be an unforeseen national emergency that might possibly convince me that it was my duty to stay on.

From the reports that come in to me, there appears to be no doubt that the dominant influence in the Democratic Party has come to be the CIO [Congress of Industrial Organizations], or at least the CIO and the AFofL [American Federation of Labor] in combination. I am told that labor unions were by far the greatest contributors to the Democrats in the recent campaign, and if you will consider the political complexion of most of the people that the Democrats put up for the Senate in the last election, you will realize that they are obviously wooing the leftish vote. Yorty, Neuberger, Taylor, Carroll, Murray, O'Mahoney, Humphrey, Douglas, MacNamara—all have the reputation of favoring big paternalistic government and centralization of political power in Washington.[1]

In view of all this, it would appear that the rift between the Southern and Northern Democrats would widen markedly, but so great is the politician's thirst for power and personal prestige that philosophical and doctrinal differences are unimportant to partisans seeking office.

We have some splendid Southern Senators—George, Byrd, Robertson, Stennis, Price Daniel, Holland and Russell are examples of the kind of men that we should have in Washington.[2] But it is almost amazing to realize that they are of the same political party as the others named above.

Yet this yawning chasm between the two wings of the Democratic Party does not appear to the public to be so formidable or paradoxical as does the much more publicized but less significant division in the Republican Party. In the Republicans you find no extreme leftists. [Wayne L.] Morse [a Republican Senator from Oregon who switched to the Democrats in 1952] deserted—thank goodness! We have what I like to call Progressive Moderates and the Conservative Rightists. However, these two groups often work in unison on important matters, notably national security, taxes, farm legislation, and so on. But our trouble has been that all of our constructive work accomplished through the support of practically every Republican in the Senate and in the House (with help from

1. The Democrats to whom Eisenhower referred were California Congressman Samuel W. Yorty, Sen. Richard L. Neuberger of Oregon, former Sen. Glen H. Taylor of Idaho, Congressman and later Sen. John A. Carroll of Colorado, Sen. James E. Murray of Montana, Sen. Joseph C. O'Mahoney of Wyoming, Sen. Hubert H. Humphrey of Minnesota, Sen. Paul H. Douglas of Illinois, and Sen. Pat McNamara of Michigan.

2. The southern senators to whom Eisenhower referred were Walter F. George and Richard B. Russell of Georgia, Harry Flood Byrd and A. Willis Robertson of Virginia, John C. Stennis of Mississippi, Price Daniel of Texas, and Spessard L. Holland of Florida.

Democrats of like convictions) has been overshadowed by the headline value of the McCarthy argument, the TVA filibuster, and the Bricker Amendment debates. These have come to mean "Republicanism" to far too many people.

The average level of ability, dedication and integrity is invariably higher in the Cabinet than it is among the politicians, where we find so many demagogues. The reason is that Cabinet members are selected person by person, normally on the basis of experience, ability, character, and standing in their several communities. This is the way mine were chosen! Others attain office through many means and methods—sometimes they are far from representative of America's best qualities. So it is lucky for a President that he is enabled to associate much more intimately with his own Cabinet than he does with politicians in general.

It is astonishing how infrequently anything of a partisan character is mentioned in the Cabinet; problems are discussed objectively and argument proceeds on the basis of bringing to bear every viewpoint on the specific project. Two of my most trusted advisors were, up until a few years ago, dyed-in-the-wool Southern Democrats. Yet this fact is one that I believe rarely occurs to any of the members of the Cabinet as we try to work out composite solutions for specific problems.

Incidentally, one of these old Democrats but now a Republican—Bob Anderson of Texas—is just about the ablest man that I know anywhere. He would make a splendid President of the United States, and I do hope that he can be sufficiently publicized as a young, vigorous Republican so that he will come to the attention of Republican groups in every state in the union. Another fine man is Herbert Hoover, Jr. In addition there are Dick Nixon, Cabot Lodge, Herb Brownell and Charlie Halleck. Some still believe that Harold Stassen has a political future, but others think he has more or less eliminated himself from serious consideration by the Republican Party as its future standard bearer.

Incidentally, there is one fact pertinent to a second term candidacy that many people seem to have overlooked. It is a tradition in this country that the moment a President publicly announces his determination not to seek re-election, his political influence disappears. From that day onward the leaders of his own party jockey for position in the hope of becoming his successor in the Presidency, while newspapers and the opposing party alike

138

lose interest in him because of his self elimination from the political future of the country.

Now here is the particular point I bring to your attention. We now have a constitutional amendment prohibiting to any man more than two terms as President. *Consequently, any President who is elected for a second term has, on that date, been officially and irrevocably eliminated as a future candidate—and presumably as a real political influence.*

The implication of this fact and this assumption is that only the most unusual of circumstances should induce any man to stand a second time for the Presidency.

Not long ago my old friend Winston [Churchill] reached the venerable age of four score. The occasion was made one of celebration throughout the Empire, and our own papers were filled with reminiscent accounts of his experiences and accomplishments. Some of these were, I thought, both reasonable and accurate; others extravagant. In reflecting on some of the statements made, I began in my own mind to arrange in priority of "greatness" the people I have known.

This is an interesting mental exercise because first one is compelled to define for himself the qualities and circumstances that enter into his own evaluations. (I have got the uneasy feeling that I may have talked on this subject to you before. If so, you can skip the next few paragraphs.)

I have long believed that no man can be classed as great unless:

a. He is either so pre-eminent in some broad field of human thought or endeavor as to have earned this classification by common acclaim

or . . .

b. He has, in some position of great responsibility, so discharged his duties as to have left a marked and favorable imprint upon the future of the society or civilization of which he is a part.

Plato would be an example of the first classification; George Washington of the second.

Greatness, of course, does not necessarily mean perfection. But I do think we have to make a distinction between a great man and a great specialist, as, for example, a great general.

Martin Luther was a great man; Napoleon was a great general. Indeed the latter had some of the qualities of a great man, but had obvious and glaring defects.

139

The qualities we seek in a great man would be vision, integrity, courage, understanding, the power of articulation either in the spoken or the written form, and what we might call profundity of character. The great specialist would be measured, I think, largely by results.

Now Churchill. Unquestionably he is a great politician and a great war leader. In addition, he has displayed many of the qualities of a great man. For my part, I think I would say that he comes nearest to fulfilling the requirements of greatness in any individual that I have met in my lifetime. I have known finer and greater characters, wiser philosophers, more understanding personalities. But they did not achieve prominence either through carrying on duties of great responsibility or through giving to the world new thoughts and ideas of such character as to bring to them by popular acclaim the title of great.

Of course I remember the old proverb that "the prophet is not without honor, save in his own country." So I think that almost any of us is more likely to call a man great if we have known him only slightly or through casual reading than we are if we have been well acquainted with him personally or studied him too long. Yet three Americans whose lives most of us have studied fairly thoroughly stand up well against all these tests, even though each had his admitted weaknesses. They are Washington, Lincoln and Robert E. Lee. Some would add Jefferson and maybe Wilson.

Of Americans I have known *personally*, I think that George Marshall possessed more of the qualities of greatness than has any other. [Chancellor Konrad] Adenauer, of Germany, ranks high on my list. And Henry L. Stimson [former secretary of state and war] was another. Among those that the Congress had produced (now I am talking again of those of whom I have read as well as those I have known), I think John Quincy Adams would head my list. In his later years, Arthur [H.] Vandenberg [senator from Michigan] came close, and in his prime I think that Senator [Walter F.] George [Dem., Ga.] likewise did so.

In any event, one is struck by the fact that two centuries have produced but few individuals who we can without any hesitation put into the classification of great. All this is of no interest, but it does give you some understanding of the thoughts that began wandering aimlessly through my mind this morning as I have dictated between appointments. These included an appointment with an official of the Pocket Testament League, the President of

Eisenhower and United States Chief of Staff George C. Marshall in Algeria, 3 June 1943 (United States Army photograph, courtesy of Dwight D. Eisenhower Library).

Saint Louis University, a new Minister from the Rumanian People's Republic, and the Ambassador of Honduras.

If there is any association of ideas between the things I have jotted down for you here and the presence of these individuals in my office this morning, I could not possibly trace it or explain it. Maybe you can.

In any event, give my love to the family, and, of course, all the best to yourself.

As ever,

P.S. I hope that my observation about greatness and its scarcity did not sound pessimistic. Long ago I learned to look for caliber or relative size in individuals rather than for perfection. So perhaps it is enough to say that with the principal officials of the Executive Department I am more than pleased. I am highly gratified with their performance and I should say that if today I could without question or confusion change any or all members of this organization, I would not remove more than two or three at the outside. Even in these cases I could not be too sure that a change would be an improvement.

1955

In December, Eisenhower sent to Swede copies of a recently completed portrait of himself and of a painting of Washington that Eisenhower himself had done. In January 1955 he returned to the subject of better pay, housing, and health benefits for members of the armed services, a rather ironic discussion given his own strong opposition to the national-health-care proposals of the Truman administration. And in an afterword, he discusses, briefly, his son's somewhat reluctant decision to remain in the army.

28 January 1955

Dear Swede:

It will probably be some time before I answer your letter in the detail that such a thoughtful communication deserves. However, I want to remark upon one point you brought up—a raise in pay for the Services.

I have personally conducted quite a survey among a number of young officers and enlisted men as to what particular thing would add most to the attractiveness of a service career for them. Of course, a number have just said, "Raise my pay." But when the subject is pursued further, much more comes to light, and, out of all this, I have concluded about as follows:

(a) A raise in pay is badly needed for highly trained technicians and non-commissioned officers in the enlisted grades.

(b) A *selective* raise in pay for officers should be enacted, particularly for those in the Army grades of Second Lieutenant to Major inclusive, and similar grades in the other Services.

(c) Some raise in pay for "hazardous duty" is needed. Since a great portion of this pay goes to aviators and submariners—and these are principally in the grades just indicated—there would be a dual raise in pay for many officers of the grades of Second Lieutenant to Major.

(d) For officers of the career services, there should be adequate quarters.

(e) For all officers of all grades, there should be fewer changes of station. These always occasion a drain upon the private purse and create a recurring necessity of fitting out homes and making new friends.

(f) Each officer should be assured decent and adequate medical care for dependents. This is particularly important these days because a young officer is so often ordered away on tours of duty of three months to a year in duration and forbidden to take his family with him. Without exception, the younger married officers I have seen give this as one of the most depressing things they encounter in Service today.

(g) There should be better provisions made for the care of dependents upon an officer's death, whether he is on the active or the retired list—in the first case, it would be a higher pension. (As of this moment, a reserve officer's widow gets something on the order of 5 or 6 times as much as a regular officer's widow if both officers die while on active service.) Likewise, retirement pay should contain a survivor's clause which would provide a minimum standard of living for his widow.

Income taxes, so far as I can see, are never again going back to the comfortable 3 or 4 percent that we paid in our early years of service. Consequently, in the average case, for every three cents added to an officer's pay, he returns one to the Federal Government. But this is not the case in what you call the "fringe" benefits.

I've had a number of Service officers conducting similar surveys and their findings largely confirm my own. But as to the basic issue, I endorse your thought, ". . . We *must* make the career services more attractive."

Thanks for your letter.

As ever,

P.S. In this matter I had a curious reaction from my son. Of course, his case is *not* typical; both he and his wife are Service "brats," he has from his grandparents some financial help and prospects and, because of me, feels a certain special obligation to the Service.

When a large firm offered him a most attractive position, he said to me:

(a) The Services are losing many young officers because of low pay and allowances, and domestic hardships.

(b) I'm in a bit better financial position to stay than is the average.

(c) If I'm any good, the Service needs me.

(d) If I'm no good, the Service will eventually fire me—as it should—but in any case I would not be existing on the charity of a business firm or friend extended to me because of my parents.

(e) So far as Service Public Relations are concerned, I think it would be unfortunate for the son of the President to resign.

In February, Eisenhower sent to Swede a brief greeting on his "non-existent" leap-year birthday. Then, in June he returned again to the possibility of his candidacy in 1956 and to a review of the accomplishments of the first several years of his presidency. Among the "definite victories" the administration had scored were Iran and Guatemala, where the Central Intelligence Agency (CIA) had toppled existing governments. The "stalemate" was Korea; and the "limited loss" was Indochina, where the French and the Vietminh had agreed to a temporary partition at the seventeenth parallel.

In his catalogue of domestic triumphs, Eisenhower obviously avoided mention of the administration's inept handling of the new poliomyelitis vaccine, which led to the resignation of the secretary of the Department of Health, Education and Welfare, Oveta Culp

Hobby, or to the Dixon-Yates scandal, which undermined his efforts to limit the TVA.

The "London Agreements" to which Eisenhower alludes brought West Germany into NATO, finally accomplishing what the United States had earlier attempted through the abortive European Defense Community. The "Big Four" meeting, coming shortly after the ascension to power of Nikita Khrushchev in the Soviet Union, did indeed signal a relaxation of East/West tensions, and for at least a brief while, both East and West basked in the "spirit of Geneva."

---

4 June 1955

Personal

Dear Swede:

A thousand things engage my attention these days, but—largely through a bombardment by loyal and well-meaning friends—the one that dominates all others is "1956." Some time ago, probably in 1953, I gave you an outline of my intentions with respect to my future in politics. Those intentions have undergone no significant change whatsoever. But as the tension mounts and the bombardment continues, the question that I will have to face next spring will be: "Are the conditions actually prevailing in the world and at home sufficiently serious as to be classed as an emergency which should properly override any personal decision or desire?"

As of this moment I feel no qualms as to my ability to hold out in what I think to be a sane and proper determination, formulated in the light of the good of the whole country. No man has ever reached his 70th year in the White House; this may not mean much in itself, but it does remind us that every Presidential term is for four years and no one has the faintest right to consider acceptance of a nomination unless he honestly believes that his physical and mental reserves will stand the strain of four years of intensive work. Incidentally, this inspires the observation that the greater the tensions of the domestic and world situation, the greater would be the erosion in mental and physical resistance.

In any event, if I should come to feel any weakening of my own resolution in this whole affair, I may get you on the phone. You are one of the very few who has seemed, from the beginning, to have been on *my* side in such matters.

The past two years or more have shown tremendous progress in procuring legislation that has been needed. This had included a new farm program, reforms in tax systems, a marked increase in pay of the uniformed services, a bill for increased pay and reform in the postal services, enactment of a better trade law and, of course, many others, particularly in the field of social security, unemployment insurance and so on. On top of all this, we have had a major tax reduction—the largest single reduction in our history—and if nothing unforeseen occurs, we approach a balanced budget, Possibly the greatest accomplishment has been the stabilization in the purchasing power of the dollar. The cost of living has varied only in the range of something like one half of one percent in the past two years.

In the international field the record is not all that we could hope, but it still shows tremendous improvement. In January of '52 Korea, Indo-China, Iran, Egypt and Guatemala all presented problems of the most acute character, some even carrying the possibility of major war. There is no need to recite here what happened in each case, but in at least three we had definite victories and of the others, a stalemate in one and limited loss in the other.

Added to all these there is the great accomplishment of the ratification of the London Agreements. The record is one to give ground for hope of greater things still to come.

Personally I do not expect any spectacular results from the forthcoming "Big Four" Conference. Nevertheless, I should think that Foster and I should be able to detect whether the Soviets really intend to introduce a tactical change that could mean, for the next few years at least, some real easing of tensions. If we do not obtain some concrete evidence of such a tactical change, then, of course, the effort must be to determine the exact purpose of recent Soviet suggestions for conferences and easing of tensions and so on.

In any event, the general world and domestic outlook is better than it was two and a half years ago.

Along with this, of course, my associates and I hope to recreate in this country some respect for constitutional methods and procedures in government, and renewed confidence in personal initiative and responsibility as the indispensable foundation of free government. I think that this also is being done.

Possibly all that I am trying to say is that if I had any special or particular function and duty in our national life in 1952, that such special duty has been or is being—so far as current circumstances will allow us to judge—largely fulfilled.

Of course I believe that prospects as of some ten months from now will be even better than at present. I hope that we will be prosperous, fully employed, and with a growing confidence in our own security and general international position. In such circumstances, I doubt that even the most demagoguish of New Dealers could induce our citizens to abandon the course on which we are now embarked so long as we could present to them as candidates, worthy representatives of "moderate conservatism."

Give my love to Ibby and all the family.

As ever,

After his return from Geneva and the adjournment of Congress, Eisenhower left Washington for Denver and an extended vacation. The question of his candidacy, however, as his letters to Swede and others indicate, remained uppermost in his mind.

There was more to the replacement of Adm. Robert B. Carney as chief of naval operations than Eisenhower's letter to Swede suggests. In late March 1955, in the midst of the tense crisis over the Chinese offshore islands of Quemoy and Matsu, Carney had told a group of reporters that war was imminent and that some in the military were pressing the president "to destroy Red China's military potential and thus end its expansionist tendencies." Eisenhower moved swiftly to quash such speculation, and two months later he had Carney quietly replaced as CNO.

Dear Swede:

This is my first day in Denver and I have a half hour to myself while waiting for an appointment with the Mayor and one or two other people. For some days I have been wanting to write to you—first to answer your intriguing letter of June 8, second to tell you something of my Geneva impressions.

Incidentally, mere mention of the date on which your letter was written takes my mind back eleven years, to June 8, 1944. That morning I visited all our landing beaches which we had struck the previous day; before the day was over I was in a first class shipwreck. I hit a sand bar—and stuck on it—at 33 knots.

A goodly portion of your letter was an analysis of the various reasons pro and con that will affect my decision about running again and the pressures that will be brought to bear—some of them spurious—by those who believe that I should do so. Of course some of this urging will come from people who merely believe that with my name on the ticket they can themselves do better politically; others, I like to believe, will be moved by real (even if possibly mistaken) concern for the country.

By and large I agree with what you have to say about age. You treat it as a relative rather than an absolute matter, and to a certain extent this is true. There is, however, one insidious factor in this matter which you do not mention. It is this. Normally the last person to recognize that a man's mental faculties are fading is the victim himself.

Exactly one week later.

I shall not attempt to explain the hiatus just indicated. It was one of those things that happen.

* * *

To return to my subject. I have seen many a man "hang on too long" under the definite impression that he had a great duty to perform and that no one else could adequately fill his particular position. The more important and demanding the position, the greater the danger in this regard.

As to who relieves me, I do not believe the question can be answered now, nor four years from this date, if I should then be at the helm.

The fact is that only the designation of a Presidential nominee *by a political convention* can glaringly focus national political attention upon any individual. For two and a half years I have genuinely tried to place two or three of our able younger men constantly before the public in the hope of giving them the publicity value that would compare favorably with their abilities. The inertia and indifference that I have encountered are scarcely less than phenomenal.

On the other hand, whoever heard of Stevenson before he was nominated? Yet today he is the tacitly acknowledged leader of the Democratic Party. What I am getting at is that no one can make accurate judgment as to the kind of political race an individual will run until *after* he is nominated. That is not wholly true in the negative sense. By this I mean that you could name dozens who could get nowhere. On the other hand, I am sure that I could name at least eight or ten Republicans, any one of whom could, by reason of personality, ability and energy, conduct a most effective campaign in our country.

So I feel that your question as to a possible successor is unanswerable, but if I should be a second term President I argue that even four years from now the question would still be unanswerable.

Of course, now, with a Constitutional amendment prohibiting a third term, the interest in a second term President would begin to die out very seriously after about the first eighteen months. All attention would be turned to the "heir apparent." This situation might in fact bring out two or three individuals who would stand out so much above the crowd that the choice could be narrowed that far.

At least I feel that the absence of an obvious successor provides no valid reason for my considering a second term.

Your concern lest I allow the rantings of an "Eager Beaver from Tennessee" to disturb me may be instantly dismissed. I never read them. In fact, there are so few people who have any real conception of the need and difficulty of keeping "fit" in this position that I pay no slightest attention to any advisory comments as to my efforts in that direction.

My reactions to Geneva have been fairly well publicized. It was difficult indeed to reach a decision that I should go to such a meeting. The twin dangers of encouraging either complacency or defeatism, depending upon the outcome, were very great indeed.

These, however, were lessened by the Soviet agreement to the Austrian Treaty, by their invitation to Adenauer to come to Moscow—after having previously threatened the most dire consequences in the event that the Paris Agreements [formally approving the inclusion of West Germany into NATO] were signed—and finally the general attitude of the new Kremlin masters: all of these encouraged the belief that possibly a new attitude might be developed in the conduct of foreign relations.

On our side, we were careful to state we were looking for nothing more, on a short term basis.

The general results you know so well as to need no elaborate comment from me. However, I am quite sure that the October meeting of the Foreign Ministers in Geneva will begin to tell the true story. But a long time must elapse before developments can possibly reach the stage that we can have any confidence in the announced purposes and proposals of the Soviets. In the meantime we must keep up our guard.

As for the change in the office of CNO, I think no one doubted the intelligence and general capacity of Admiral Carney. But I know that a very distinct difference in philosophies affecting naval direction and authority arose between him and the Secretary of the Navy [Charles S. Thomas]. Personally, I think there is nothing complicated about the line of authority and responsibility. The President is Commander in Chief. He delegates to a Service Secretary a certain amount of his Constitutional authority and that Secretary becomes the President's representative in the affected service. The Secretary's orders are presumed to be the orders of the Commander in Chief. If the Secretary is the type who does not take the advice of his own military choices, or who is domineering and arbitrary in his decisions, then it is the fault of the Commander in Chief for having selected such a person, if things go wrong—as they surely would.

But the theory that the control and direction of all parts of the Navy fall within the responsibility and authority of the Secretary cannot be questioned, even though the CNO has an additional capacity as the chief "Naval Adviser to the President." As I understand the matter, from both sides, (and of course this a highly secret) Carney holds that there are certain matters within the direction and operation of the Naval chiefs, with which the Secretary has no possible concern or right to interfere.

I would go so far as to say that if the Secretary felt it necessary to interfere, then he should instantly relieve the CNO. However, the only way he can know what is going on is to be constantly informed and to demand and have all the inspectional rights as to operations, reports, communications and so on, which are necessary to him in order to form his own judgment in these matters. Unless this is so, there could be no control over any CNO—certainly the President has no time to check up on such details.

By no means do I intend to imply that the difference was carried to the point of acrimonious debate or any kind of insubordination. However, I believe it was serious enough that the Secretary was no longer too happy with the current situation and therefore recommended the change. Without exception all of us think that Thomas has been a good Secretary, so in the circumstances it seemed best to make the change.

With warm regard,

As ever,

Early on the morning of 24 September 1955, Eisenhower suffered a severe heart attack and was rushed to a nearby military hospital. In Washington there was anxious talk of constitutional succession. In New York the Dow-Jones industrial average fell more than thirty points. For the next several weeks the president remained in virtual seclusion, shielded by his physicians, by Assistant to the President Sherman Adams, and by his trusted press secretary, James C. Hagerty. "Welcome to the Cardiac Club," wrote Swede on September 27, in a determinedly cheerful letter. Eisenhower's reply, dictated on October 6, was accompanied by a note from his private secretary, Ann C. Whitman, who passed along a request from Hagerty that it not be made public. "It is one of two dictated by him today," she wrote, "and of course the newspapers would love nothing better than to know about it." Whitman went on to assure Swede that Eisenhower's progress was, if anything, underestimated. "He looks wonderfully well, he

Eisenhower at Fitzsimmons Army Hospital, Denver, Colorado, 25 October 1955 (by permission of United Press International).

is relaxed and cheerful—and he promises to be a good patient. More than that we cannot ask!''

---

6 October 1955

Dear Swede:

While the doctors have almost completely succeeded in ''divorcing'' me from my secretary (and thus effectively prevented the kind of reply I should like to make to your note), they relented

152

sufficiently to allow me a moment to tell you how much I appreciated your letter. It was the best possible therapy.

As soon as possible, I want to write you fully. Meantime, my warm and grateful thanks.

With affectionate regard to Ibby, and, as always, the best to yourself.

As ever,

"But of course you won't run—and I'm glad," wrote Swede on October 21, reminding Eisenhower that he had once written that he considered his brother Milton the best fitted of anyone in the country to serve as president. "I think he is a natural," Swede concluded, "and the Eisenhower name alone will pull a lot of votes." In his reply, Eisenhower reiterated his high regard for his younger brother's abilities but also repeated his conviction that Milton had no interest in "politics."

---

26 October 1955

Personal and Confidential

Dear Swede:

I shall not attempt fully to answer your very fine letter, but, regarding the paragraph at the top of your second page, which deals with the "hands off" attitude with regard to a successor, let us *not* forget this one thing. I am vitally concerned in seeing someone nominated who not only believes in the program I have been so earnestly laboring to have enacted into law, but who also has the best chance of election. This is the tough one.

With regard to Milton, I have not changed my mind one iota. In fact, my judgment of past years has been strengthened with every new day. But what might ever come of my own opinion in this matter is something that I have not even seriously considered. Certainly this is no time for anyone to make any kind of a move. In fact, it is my own private opinion that if ever there is a fight to develop in this world between my kid brother and myself, it will be when and if he ever finds out that I would like to see him shoved into politics in this fashion.

Today I am walking a few steps. The doctors say my progress follows the normal pattern. With your experience you know, I assume, exactly what that means. Apparently there is a period of some four months before they can make an accurate prognosis of the level of activity a heart victim can sustain without incurring any damage. By that time a lot of factors that now appear doubtful or uncertain should definitely crystallize.

Give my love to Ibbie.

As ever,

On December 19 a friend of Swede's from California wrote Eisenhower that Swede "has been having a rough time and I just wasn't sure he had admitted to you how rough." Eisenhower immediately dictated the following letter. Later, after hearing from Swede, he had Ann Whitman write to the friend that while Swede's condition was "not good of course, it is apparently no worse than it has been for some time."

---

23 December 1955

Dear Swede:

It seems much too long since I have heard of you, and with the approaching holiday season I feel once again the necessity of being in touch—even if it must be by letter—with you.

I find that my last letter was dated October twenty-sixth, and its principal topic, still unresolved, swirls daily around my mind and keeps me awake at nights. At the moment I don't want to mar the holiday season—and my exhilarated state of mind at being a grandfather for the fourth time—with delving into the matter too deeply in a letter.

As far as my physical condition is concerned, I seem to be making the progress the doctors have anticipated. The one thing I need is exercise, but the weather at Gettysburg was too uncomfortable to permit me to be out very much—and while I can get a reasonable amount of exercise in the gymnasium here, the activities are not really those I most enjoy. I would like to go south for a couple of weeks, but there are certain family considerations which have priority.

I am afraid that I have had far too great a preoccupation with my own health these past months. More importantly, what about you? I would very much like to know how you are feeling and whether or not you are getting the treatment you need.

The other day I sent you one of the lithographic reproductions of a painting I did the last week I spent in Fraser. I hope you and Ibby like it.

This rambling letter represents nothing more, as I say, than a desire to be in touch with you and, specifically, to inquire about your health.

Give my love to Ibby and, as always, the best to yourself.

As ever,

1956

Reassured somewhat as to the state of Swede's health, Eisenhower launched into a long discussion of his own regimen and of the still unresolved question of his candidacy.

23 January 1956

Personal and Confidential

Dear Swede:

I was more than delighted to have your letter. It had been some time since you had written to me, and I had begun to grow fearful you were feeling badly and that correspondence was too much of a drain on your strength. So when I found I had two or three pages of pure "Swede," I experienced a great lift, even before I had started its reading.

From your letter I see that I must have previously mentioned some of the difficulties I have in sleeping. Let me assure you that I have no trouble at all going to sleep. For a matter of five hours or so I sleep as well as I ever did in my life. But ever since the hectic days of the North African campaign, I find that when I have weighty matters on my mind I wake up extremely early, apparently because a rested mind is anxious to begin grappling with knotty questions.

Incidentally, I never worry about what I did the day before. Likewise, I spend no time fretting about what enemies or critics have said about me. I have never indulged in useless regrets. Always I find, when I have come awake sufficiently to figure out what may be then engaging my attention, that I am pondering some question that is still unanswered.

So I think it is fair to say that it is not worry or useless anxiety about the past, but a desire to attack the future that gets me into this annoying habit.

On the whole, however, I think I do pretty well in the matter of rest. Almost every day, since my attack, I have gotten a nap ranging from a few minutes to more than an hour. In addition to this, I certainly must average (because sometimes I do go back to sleep for a while after an early awakening) some six to six and a half hours at night. A fellow my age ought to get along all right on the aggregate.

Incidentally, you might be interested in what Dr. [Paul Dudley] White has to say about mid day rest. He is very much against lying prone *after* lunch. He insists that I lie down at least a half hour before luncheon, and does not seem to be too much concerned whether I actually go to sleep. After lunch he insists that I take an hour's rest in an easy chair, but I must not lie down. During this hour in the chair, he has no objection to my conversing with a friend or reading papers that are not too full of argumentative features.

My exercise is supposed to include a short swim in a warm pool each day, a walk of some half hour (this I have almost wholly neglected since returning from the south), climbing of one full set of stairs of about twenty steps, and several sessions of swinging my golf clubs even when I am not attempting to play outdoors.

I am supposed to take ten minutes each hour out of every long conference and to leave the room and either lie or sit down by myself, allowing nothing to disturb me. Likewise, I am to avoid all situations that tend to bring about such reactions as irritation, frustration, anxiety, fear and, above all, anger. When doctors give me such instructions, I say to them, "Just what do you think the Presidency is?" Finally, the instruction that I simply have not learned to keep is "eat slowly." For some reason I have never been able just to sit leisurely at a table and take my time enjoying food. I am always hungry as a bear when I sit down and I show it. For forty years I have been a trial to Mamie. She has done her best, but she still has made little impression.

As I have tried to tell so many people, I do not think it is of any great importance just what this job might do to me as an individual. I recognize that men are mortal. Moreover, during the war there were sometimes situations involving decisions compelling temporary and occasionally fairly acute personal danger. I had to become sufficiently objective to realize that great causes, movements and programs not only outlive, but are far more important than the individuals who may be their respective leaders.

But I do think people ought to give a little more thought to what the failing health of a President might do to the office and to the cause for which a whole Administration could be working.

We well know that when advancing years and diminishing energy begin to take their toll, the last one that ever appreciates such a situation is the victim himself. Consequently, he can slow up operations, impede the work of all his subordinates, and by so doing, actually damage the cause for which he may even think he is giving some years of his life. (And loyal subordinates will not break his heart by telling him of his growing unfitness—they just *try* to make up for it.)

Also, let us remember that at this moment we are not trying to guess how I will feel *next* January twentieth with respect to four future years, after I have had a full year to make my own conclusions. Right now, still only four months after the first heart attack that ever hit the Eisenhower family, I have soon to decide what is my answer with respect to the *next five years*.

It is all very complicated, and I could fill any number of pages with the various considerations pro and con that I think have some bearing on the matter.

In any event, it was wonderful to read about your activities and to note that you are going strong.

Give my love to Ibby and the children, and, of course, always the best to yourself.

As ever,

Despite his frequently stated intention not to run in 1956, despite the clear absence of any threatening international emergency (such as he had suggested, at one point, might cause him to reconsider), despite his advancing age (he would turn sixty-six in October), and in spite of the heart attack he had suffered the preceding fall, Eisenhower nevertheless decided to run again for the presidency, a decision that he announced in late February. This is, despite the many disclaimers, the letter of a man who fully enjoyed the power and prestige of the presidency and who, indeed, was prepared to fight, if necessary, to retain it.

---

2 March 1956

Personal and Confidential

Dear Swede:

The whole tough business of making up my mind to bow my neck to what seemed to be the inevitable; of then deciding how and when to make my announcement as to a second term; and finally the intensive work of preparing notes from which to speak to the American people, has so occupied my mind and days that I simply had no chance to carry out my hope of writing to you in advance to tell you all about it.

Even the giving of my consent, in 1952, to stand for the Republican nomination was not as difficult as was the decision to lay my name again before that convention. I suppose there are no two people in the world who have more than Mamie and I earnestly wanted, for a number of years, to retire to their home—a home which we did not even have until a year or so ago.

When I first rallied from my attack of September twenty-fourth, I recall that almost my first conscious thought was "Well, at least this settles one problem for me for good and all."

For five weeks I was not allowed to see a newspaper or to listen to a radio. While, within a matter of a week after I was stricken, I took up the practice of daily meetings with Governor [Sherman] Adams and gradually increased my contacts with other members of the staff and the Administration, the doctors still kept the newspapers away for the reason they didn't want me worried about stories and gossip concerning my illness.

On top of this, I found it something of a relief to be away from the daily doings of the world, and consequently I did my work from knowledge already acquired, and from official reports, memoranda and studies brought to me by associates.

As a consequence of this hiatus in my understanding of what was going on in the world, I was astounded when I found that even as early as early November a great number of people were saying that they believed I could and should run again! I had a letdown feeling that approached a sense of frustration. As I look back, I truly believe that could I have anticipated in early October what later public reaction was going to be, I would have probably issued a short statement to the effect that I would determine as soon as possible whether it was physically possible for me *to finish out this term, but that I would thereafter retire from public life.*

Having missed the opportunity to do this (and again I say I cannot be so certain that I would have done it), it seemed to me that I had no recourse but patiently to wait the outcome of all the tests the doctors wanted to make on me and gradually come to a decision myself as to whether or not I could stand the pace.

I wish I could tell you just exactly what finally made me decide as I did, but there was such a vast combination of circumstances and factors that seemed to me to have a bearing on the problem— and at times the positive and negative were delicately balanced— that I cannot say for certain which particular one was decisive.

One—and this has been mentioned to no one else—had to do with a guilty feeling on my own part that I had failed to bring forward and establish a logical successor for myself. This failure was of course not intentional. To the contrary, I struggled hard to acquaint the public with the qualities of a very able group of young men; I will not bore you with the repetition of the story I told you many months ago. But the evidence became clear that I had not been able to get any individual to be recognized as a natural or logical candidate for the Presidency.

Parenthetically, I have just about decided that a first-term President—unless he has been publicly repudiated from the beginning of his term—can scarcely get his own party to think in terms of a candidate other than himself.

Of course, I told my story as much as I could over the television, the other evening, but in any such presentation it was obviously impossible even to refer to all the types and kinds of influences that seemed important.

For example, I think we have put together in the Executive Branch, the ablest group of civilians that has worked in government during the long years I have been around Washington. If I had quit, no matter who might be elected in my place, there would be a tendency for this band to scatter. After all, two or three of them are even older than I, and most of them have business affairs and interests that attract them to a freer existence than they can lead here.

There was a volume of mail from people who almost prayerfully hoped that I would consider the matter favorably. Only two or three of my friends really urged me to decline, and all of these put the matter purely on the personal basis—that I would shorten my life. Possibly this is so. But it is certainly true that never once in all these weeks of study has it occurred to me that that particular point was of great importance.

There remain several questions about the *current year*.

The first is that if I am to have a recurrence of this illness, I assume that the possibility is greater during this year than it will be during any one of the following two or three. In my case this would seem to be true if for no other reason than because, in an election year, the tirades of demagogues and the newspaper quarrels tend to reach a venomous level. In fact, if one were not rather philosophical about the things he reads and hears, any sensitive man would never attain that calmness of attitude and spirit that the cardiologists so glibly talk about.

Finally, I am a competitor, a fighter, so if, as normally happens, politicians begin to get scared along about the middle of October and see themselves losing the election because of lack of activity on my part, my own reluctance ever to accept defeat might tempt me into activity that should be completely eliminated from my life.

This I shall, of course, earnestly try to resist, but politicians are funny people and they can certainly paint a situation ''scary'' when they get to worrying about an election.

When I consider how many times I have been driven away from personal plans, I sometimes think that I must be a very weak character. I think that one mistake I made was in assuming, in 1948, that I had forever destroyed the possibility of a political career for myself. When I finally, in January of '52, acknowledged publicly that I was a Republican, I realized that I had gone a long ways away from the personal objectives that Mamie and I had laid down for ourselves. Having gotten into the struggle, however, I naturally was not going to take any chances of defeat that I could avoid. I worked hard.

The next time that I had a defeat of a similar kind was when I allowed myself to be talked out of my purpose of announcing, in my Inaugural Address, that I was a one-term President only. However, all of the people who persuaded me to do so agreed that, at my age, one term was all that should be expected of me, or that I should attempt. My recent decision represents another of the same kind of defeat—speaking only from the personal viewpoint. I have gotten to the point that I believe the Constitutional Amendment limiting Presidential tenure to two terms is a good one, even though, logically, I think it is indefensible.

Far more than balancing all of this is the hope that I may still be able to do something in promoting mutual confidence, and therefore peace, among the nations. And that I can help our people understand that they must avoid extremes in reaching solutions to the social, economic and political problems that are constantly with us. If I could be certain that my efforts would really promote these two things, I shall certainly never have any cause for sympathizing with myself—no matter what happens.

I have talked enough and I have probably not clarified for you a single thing that was causing you doubt; possibly I have not even added an atom of information to your own store of knowledge. But I feel better for having written. I am fortunate in having you to absorb some of the offshoots from my sometimes wandering mind—and to get your reactions.

Give my love to Ibby and the family.

As ever,

On the evening of 7 June 1956, Eisenhower suffered an attack of what his doctors now diagnosed as chronic ileitis, and on June 9 he underwent a major operation in which the diseased section of his small intestine was surgically bypassed. As with the heart attack, the president's health once more became front-page news. But also, as in the case of the heart attack, Eisenhower's vigorous constitution speeded recovery. Swede's letter to Eisenhower was acknowledged by his personal secretary, Ann Whitman. "I merely want to tell you that your letter . . . pleased him enormously and that it will be one of the things he will want to answer personally when he feels a little more like himself." She assured Swede that Eisenhower "looked rosy and not at all as though he had lost weight . . . the important thing is that from now on he won't have any more of those awful attacks. . . ." Two weeks later, she wrote again, reporting that Eisenhower was feeling much better and "getting back his zest and smiling once again that wide, wonderful smile." Eisenhower himself did not write until he and Mamie had returned to Gettysburg for a brief convalescence.

---

12 July 1956

Dear Swede:

Your letter to me in the hospital (which reached me promptly, despite my long delay in acknowledging it personally) really gave me a lift at the time it was most needed. I don't want to complain unduly, but the first days after the operation were really uncomfortable. But your reassurances, coupled with those of the doctors, buoyed my flagging spirits and got me through three very difficult weeks.

Now that I am here at Gettysburg and can detect a daily increase in strength and vitality, I am ready to put the whole nasty business behind me. The announcement [reaffirming his decision to run] which filtered out Tuesday through Senator [William F.] Knowland was an attempt to do just that.

The farm has never looked better, mainly by virtue of the frequent gentle rains we have had since we have been here, and I have been happily renewing my acquaintance with my tiny Angus herd. Official business, a small amount of "farming," and a strict regime of treatment, mild exercise and rest, more than occupy my days.

I want to write you again when I have more time to myself, but meantime I did want to tell you, before another day passed, how greatly [I appreciated] the thoughts and prayers of Ibby and yourself.

With warm regard,

As ever,

One of the first crises that Eisenhower faced after his recovery was the nationalization of the Suez Canal by Egypt's prime minister, Gamal Abdel Nasser. Even a healthy Eisenhower would have had difficulty in preventing this crisis, bred as it was by conflict between colonialism and nationalism, between Arabs and Israelis, and between the United States and the Soviet Union. As it was, during a year punctuated by both the heart attack and the ileitis operation, American blunders helped to precipitate Nasser's seizure of the canal in late July.

In Washington, meanwhile, the House of Representatives failed to approve Eisenhower's recommendation that the United States join the Organization for Trade Cooperation (OTC). Protectionists, led for the most part by conservative Republicans, charged that United States membership in the OTC would harm American industry.

---

3 August 1956

Dear Swede:

From a personal viewpoint, the past year has been notable mainly because of unaccustomed illness. It is scarcely useful, however, to make this a subject of a letter to you because my "innards" have been pictured, described and discussed in the papers, to say nothing of on the television and radio, until you, along with many others, must be heartily sick of the whole business.

Of course, the two illnesses taken together provide for partisan political opponents a very fine platform from which to "view with alarm." Such people pretend to be astonished that I have not rebounded, within seven weeks, from a major operation, to my pre-operational level of weight, strength and physical activity.

I notice that one man has gone to the trouble of figuring out that, due to my heart attack, I was 143 days absent from duty, while in the second instance he figured I added another 42, at least. Nothing is said about the fact that in Denver, within five days of my initial attack, staff officers were in my room asking for decisions, while in my latest operation I had to be functioning again in the space of three days. Actually, after an operation on Saturday morning, I sat up to receive and talk to Chancellor Adenauer for quite a visit on the following Thursday.

I am, of course, disappointed that no other Republican has come sufficiently to the fore in public opinion as to make of himself a possible Presidential candidate satisfactory to the Party. But this was true before I thought of being sick; I still believe that, had I not suffered a heart attack in September, I could have taken much more drastic steps than I did to force the Republican Party to consider and accept someone else.

All that is in the past.

Today the difficult things for me are political, both in the domestic and in the international fields. Nasser and the Suez Canal are foremost in my thoughts. Whether or not we can get a satisfactory solution for this problem and one that tends to restore rather than further to damage the prestige of the Western Powers, particularly of Britain and France, is something that is not yet resolved. In the kind of world that we are trying to establish, we frequently find ourselves victims of the tyrannies of the weak. In the effort to promote the rights of all, and observe the equality of sovereignty as between the great and the small, we unavoidably give to the little nations opportunities to embarrass us greatly. Faithfulness to the underlying concepts of freedom is frequently costly. Yet there can be no doubt that in the long run such faithfulness will produce real rewards.

One of the frustrating facts of my daily existence is the seeming inability of our people to understand our position and role in the world and what our own best interests demand of us.

The other day I happened onto a copy of Mckinley's last speech, delivered the day before he was shot. In it he argued for more and freer trade, for reciprocal trade treaties—and made the flat assertion, "Isolation is no longer possible or desirable." What he discerned 55 years ago has grown more true with every passing year, especially as we became more and more a creditor nation. Yet an astonishing number of people today believe that our welfare lies in higher tariffs, meaning greater isolation and a refusal to buy goods from others. They fail to see that no matter what we do in providing, through loans, for the urgent needs of other countries in investment capital, unless we simultaneously pursue a policy that permits them to make a living, we are doomed to eventual isolation and to the disappearance of our form of government.

Now I do not expect the trend of which I speak to go that far. Before a final disaster of this kind came upon us, there would be greater understanding of the facts and corrective action gradually applied. But I do greatly fear that this trend could continue until we might have lost certain important segments of the remaining free world—a loss which will make our future existence more difficult, and possibly even more dangerous.

Many years ago someone wrote a little novel or story, the central theme of which was that the rich owner of a factory could not forever live on top of the hill in luxury and serenity, while all around him at the bottom of the hill his workmen lived in misery, privation and resentment. In comparatively recent years we learned this lesson nationally. As a result, we have the greatest middle class in the world because there is practically nobody in the lowest or "edge of starvation" group. Now we must learn the same lesson internationally—and once having learned the lesson we must study the best ways to bring about better standards for the underdeveloped nations. It cannot be done by grants, it will not be the result of any one specific action.

We must pursue a broad and intelligent program of loans, trade, technical assistance and, under current conditions, mutual guarantees of security. We must stop talking about "give aways." We must understand that our foreign expenditures are investments in America's future. A simple example: No other nation is exhausting its irreplaceable resources so rapidly as is ours. Unless we are careful to build up and maintain a great group of international friends ready to trade with us, where do we hope to get all the materials that we will one day need as our rate of consumption continues and accelerates? Possibly the future chemist will make all the materials we need out of crops grown annually, but, if he does, that day will probably come long after our minerals of various kinds are fairly well exhausted.

It just occurs to me that I seem to be thrusting off on to you some of my problems and troubles. I didn't mean to do so, but at least you will see that in the approach to such grave difficulties as the Suez crisis, there is a great need for keeping in the back of the mind the understanding of these broader, long-term issues in the international world.

Give my love to Ibby.

As ever,

On the day before his departure for San Francisco and the Republican National Convention, Eisenhower returned to an issue that had occupied much of his attention during World War II and during his tour as chief of staff, that of interservice rivalry. It was an issue that would grow particularly intense during the second term, as the services, together with their allies in Congress and industry, lobbied for larger and larger defense expenditures. These struggles would ultimately prompt Eisenhower, in his Farewell Address, to warn of the grave dangers to the United States that were being posed by the "military-industrial complex."

---

20 August 1956

Personal and Confidential

Dear Swede:

The probable explanation for the simultaneous arrival in New York of your two letters, one bearing three cents and the other six cents postage, is the institution of a new policy on the part of the Postmaster General. Where a subsidized air line is not involved, and a three cent letter can be carried on a plane without extra cost—and space is available—the policy is to pick up the letter and carry it exactly as if it were bearing a six cent stamp.

Not long ago you expressed some of your irritation that anyone should even dream of putting the Services into the same uniform. I won't quarrel with the idea, but I will attempt to give you a slightly different viewpoint toward the Services than you probably have.

So far as I am personally concerned, I should say that my most frustrating domestic problem is that of attempting to achieve any real coordination among the Services. Time and again I have had the high Defense officials in conference—with all the senior military and their civilian bosses present—and have achieved what has seemed to me general agreement on policy and function—but there always comes the break-up. The kindest interpretation that can be put on some of these developments is that each service is so utterly confident that it alone can assure the nation's security, that it feels justified in going before the Congress or the public and urging fantastic programs. Sometimes it is by no means the heads of the Services that start these things. Some subordinate gets to going, and then a demagogue gets into the act and the Chief of the Service finds it rather difficult to say, "No, we could not profitably use another billion dollars."

What I have tried to tell the Chiefs of Staff is that their most important function is their corporate work as a body of advisers to the Secretary of Defense and to me. We now have four-star men acting as their deputies, and those men are either capable of running the day-to-day work in the Services or they should not be wearing that kind of insignia. Yet I have made little or no progress in developing real corporate thinking.

I patiently explain over and over again that American strength is a combination of its economic, moral and military force. If we demand too much in taxes in order to build planes and ships, we will tend to dry up the accumulations of capital that are necessary to provide jobs for the million or more new workers that we must absorb each year. Behind each worker there is an average of about $15,000 in invested capital. His job depends upon this investment at a yearly rate of not less than fifteen to twenty billions. If taxes become so burdensome that investment loses its attractiveness for capital, there will finally be nobody but government to build the facilities. This is one form of Socialism.

Let us not forget that the Armed Services are to defend a "way of life," not merely land, property or lives. So what I try to make the Chiefs realize is that they are men of sufficient stature, training and intelligence to think of this balance—the balance between minimum requirements in the costly implements of war and the health of our economy.

Based on this kind of thinking, they habitually, when with me, give the impression that they are going to work out arrangements that will keep the military appropriations within manageable proportions and do it in a spirit of good will and of give and take.

Yet when each Service puts down its minimum requirements for its own military budget for the following year, and I add up the total, I find that they mount at a fantastic rate. There is seemingly no end to all of this. Yet merely "getting tough" on my part is not an answer. I simply must find men who have the breadth of understanding and devotion to their country rather than to a single Service that will bring about better solutions than I get now.

Strangely enough, the one man who sees this clearly is a Navy man who at one time was an uncompromising exponent of Naval power and its superiority over any other kind of strength. That is [Adm. Arthur W.] Radford.

I do not maintain that putting all of these people in one uniform would cure this difficulty—at least not quickly. But some day there is going to be a man sitting in my present chair who has not been raised in the military services and who will have little understanding of where slashes in their estimates can be made with little or no damage. If that should happen while we still have the state of tension that now exists in the world, I shudder to think of what could happen in this country.

* * *

Tomorrow Mamie and I leave for San Francisco and what promises to be, for us at least, a hectic and tumultuous two days there. Then Cypress Point—and I *hope* some rest.

Give my love to Ibby.

As ever,

During the fall campaign, Eisenhower wrote to Swede only once, and then briefly. His secretary, Ann Whitman, also wrote to Swede a month later.

17 September 1956

Dear Swede:

I shall follow your advice and at this moment shall attempt no lengthy answer to your fine letter of the twelfth. I give you merely my own personal report on my health, which is that I really do feel splendid.

On Wednesday evening I am to make about a twenty minute talk on the Columbia Broadcasting System, and the following day I go out to Iowa where I will attend informally (and *without* a major address) the plowing contest at Newton, Iowa. Then, after returning here, I shall go out to Illinois only three or four days later to deliver a major farm speech.

Give my love to Ibby and the children, and again my thanks for your note.

With warm regard,

As ever,

22 October 1956

Dear Captain Hazlett:

You of all people will understand that for the next two weeks the President is the busiest of men. He asked me simply to thank you for your good wishes for his [sixty-sixth] birthday. Incidentally, he told me the other day his current ambition was to live until he could switch the numbers upside down!

Furthermore he said to tell you—apropos of your statement that he should not get too mad—that he had been helped a lot in this regard by golf. The doctors have insisted that he could play only if he refused to get mad at himself when he played poorly. Actually, he hasn't had a game of golf for the last five or six weeks; there just hasn't been time.

Probably you watched the President's progress through the last trip. Capsule: here it is—Minneapolis and St. Paul turned out the most tremendous crowds I have ever seen anywhere—three and four deep in residential districts (and packed on the sidewalks in the business districts); Seattle, not too many people along the motorcade route but an intensely enthusiastic audience at the Rally. [Republican senatorial candidate Arthur B.] Langlie seems to be in trouble, as incidentally, does [former Secretary of the Interior Douglas] Mckay [who resigned to challenge Democratic incumbent Wayne Morse]. Portland was again wildly enthusiastic, and of course, Los Angeles outdid itself as only that city can in screwballs and glamor and enthusiasm.

The President took the whole thing in that magnificent stride of his, while the lesser of us felt an inclination at times to fall by the wayside. But we all returned, pretty much in pieces, but here at least.

The President will write you, I know, once this whole fracas is over. Meantime, you know he is thinking of you.

Sincerely,

[Ann C. Whitman]

In regard to the Middle East, Eisenhower's repeated efforts to reach a peaceful settlement to the Suez crisis were frustrated, and Great Britain, France, and Israel began to make secret preparations for armed intervention. Their plan was for Israel to attack Egypt across the Sinai Peninsula, which would then become the pretext for an Anglo-French invasion to "protect" the canal from the two combatants, Egypt and Israel. The Israeli attack began on October

29, in the midst of a two-week period marked also by the abortive uprising in Hungary and by the election in the United States.

Eisenhower, whom the British and French had sought to deceive, responded coolly and deliberately. "We cannot and we will not condone armed aggresison," he declared, "no matter who the attacker, and no matter who the victim." When British and French troops landed at the northern end of the canal a few days later, he quickly moved to tighten economic and political pressure on his former allies. The Soviet Union, meanwhile, issued threatening warnings to Britain, France, and Israel. Faced with opposition from both Russia and the United States, the British and French soon capitulated, agreeing to a cease-fire and a negotiated withdrawal.

Meanwhile, in the election, Eisenhower won by a landslide, easily defeating Adlai Stevenson and his running mate, Tennessee's Senator Estes Kefauver. The Democrats, however, as Eisenhower seems to have anticipated, retained control of both the House and the Senate.

---

2 November 1956

PERSONAL

Dear Swede:

Except for an informal appearance on a "Round-up" telecast from 11 to 12 o'clock on Election Eve, I have finished my campaigning. It became too difficult for me to keep in touch with the various items of information that pour constantly into Washington from Europe and the Mid East and at the same time carry on the hectic activities of actual campaigning.

It is not difficult at all to operate efficiently in carrying on Presidential functions from any other point in the United States, if there is opportunity to set up the kind of communications required. But when I am gone from here for a period of eight to twelve hours, or up to two to three days, with no communications available other than commercial telephone, it becomes much more difficult, especially so with a world situation such as now exists.

But there is another reason that I decided to do no more in this campaign. Up until a few months ago, I had set my face determinedly against any campaigning except for three or four television speeches to be given in a Washington studio. Some weeks back, however, a lot of people in the Administration came to believe that the distortions and half truths peddled by Stevenson and Kefauver had to be answered—and that no speaker of ours, other than myself, could gain a sufficient audience to answer them effectively.

So I took to the speaking trail, first to call the hand of the opponents on some of the wild things they were saying, and secondly, to awaken the American people to the importance of the contest and to the realization that each of them should record his own decision.

This I think has been done. So in my last evening's talk, in Philadelphia, I confined myself to laying out the approach I have employed since 1952 to the whole problem of foreign relations and how I would approach it in the future if the American people want me to continue.

Actually, unless I win by a comfortable majority (one that could not be significantly increased or decreased in the next few days by any amount of speaking on either side), I would not want to be elected at all. This is for a few simple reasons, even though I believe that the Stevenson-Kefauver combination is, in some ways, about the sorriest and weakest we have ever had run for the two top offices in the land.

My first reason is that I still have a job of re-forming and re-vamping the Republican Party. Since by the Constitution this is my final term, my influence in these next four years with my own party is going to be determined by their feeling as to how popular I am with the multitudes. If they feel that my support will be a real asset in the next election they, individually and as a party, will be disposed to go in the direction that I advocate. If, on the contrary, they think that politically I am a rapidly "waning" star, then they would be disposed to take the bit in their teeth regardless of my opinions.

My second reason is that in any event, whether or not we win control of one or both Houses of the Congress, the division is certain to be very close. In almost every project some Democratic help will be absolutely necessary to get it accomplished. Again this strength can be marshalled, on both sides of the aisle, *only* if it is generally believed that I am in a position to go to the people over the heads of the Congressmen—and either help them or cause them trouble in their districts.

For these two reasons I think that my only opportunity for doing anything really worthwhile is to win by a comfortable majority. This belief, incidentally, was an additional reason for my deciding to do a bit of traveling in the campaign. It also offered me a chance to prove to the American people that I am a rather healthy individual.

I had planned two more trips—one for last Wednesday when I was going to stop at the airfields in Dallas, Oklahoma City and Memphis, and the other for the last day of the campaign when I expected to stop in Hartford, Connecticut, and Boston, Massachusetts. These I cancelled, mostly because of preoccupation with official business.

The Mid East thing is a terrible mess. Ever since July twenty-sixth, when Nasser took over the Canal, I have argued for a negotiated settlement. It does not seem to me that there is present in the case anything that justifies the action that Britain, France and Israel apparently concerted among themselves and have initiated.

The 1888 Treaty says nothing at all as to how the Canal is to be operated, although it did recognize the existence of the "Concession" dating, I believe, from 1868. I think, therefore, that no one could question the legal right of Egypt to nationalize the Canal *Company*. And what really became the apparent or legal bone of contention was, "Shall the world's users of the Canal, which is guaranteed as an international waterway in perpetuity, be privileged to use the Canal only on the sufferance of a single nation?" Even this, in my opinion, is not the real heart of the matter.

The real point is that Britain, France and Israel had come to believe—probably correctly—that Nasser was their worst enemy in the Mid East and that until he was removed or deflated, they would have no peace. I do not quarrel with the idea that there is justification for such fears, but I have insisted long and earnestly that you cannot resort to force in international relationships because of your fear of what might happen in the future. In short, I think the British and French seized upon a very poor vehicle to use in bringing Nasser to terms.

Of course, nothing in the region would be so difficult to solve except for the underlying cause of the unrest and dissension that exists there—that is, the Arab-Israel quarrel. This quarrel seems to have no limit either in intensity or in scope. Everybody in the Moslem and Jewish worlds is affected by it. It is so intense that the second any action is taken against one Arab state, by an outsider, all the other Arab and Moslem states seem to regard it as a Jewish plot and react violently. All this complicates the situation enormously.

As we began to uncover evidence that something was building up in Israel, we demanded pledges from [Prime Minister David] Ben-Gurion that he would keep the peace. We realized that he might think he could take advantage of this country because of the approaching election and because of the importance that so many politicians in the past have attached to our Jewish vote. I gave strict orders to the State Department that they should inform Israel that we would handle our affairs exactly as though we didn't have a Jew in America. The welfare and best interests of our own country were to be the sole criteria on which we operated.

I think that France and Britain have made a terrible mistake. Because they had such a poor case, they have isolated themselves from the good opinion of the world and it will take them many years to recover. France was perfectly cold-blooded about the matter. She has a war on her hands in Algeria, and she was anxious to get someone else fighting the Arabs on her Eastern flank so she was ready to do anything to get England and Israel in that affair. But I think the other two countries have hurt themselves immeasurably and this is something of a sad blow because, quite naturally, Britain not only has been, but must be, our best friend in the world.

Only a star-gazer could tell how the whole thing is going to come out. But I can tell you one thing. The existence of this problem does not make sleeping any easier—not merely because of the things I recite above, but because of the opportunities that we have handed to the Russians. I don't know what the final action of the United Nations on this matter will be. We are struggling to get a simple cease-fire and, with it, compulsion on both sides to start negotiations regarding the Canal, withdrawal of troops, and even proper reparations. But the possibility that both sides will accept some compromise solution does not look very bright, and every day the hostilities continue the Soviets have an additional chance to embarrass the Western world beyond measure.

All these thoughts I communicated to [Sir Anthony] Eden [British prime minister] time and again. It was undoubtedly because of his knowledge of our bitter opposition to using force in the matter that when he finally decided to undertake the plan, he just went completely silent. Actually, the British had partially dispersed some of their concentrations in the Mid East and, while we knew the trouble was not over, we did think that, so far as Britain and France were concerned, there was some easing of the situation.

Just one more thought before I close this long letter. There is some reason to believe that the plan, when actually put into effect, was not well coordinated. It looks as if the Israelis mobilized pretty rapidly and apparently got ready to attack before the others were immediately ready to follow up, using the Israeli attack as an excuse to "protect" the Canal. In any event, British and French troops, so far as I know, have not yet landed in Egypt. Apparently there has been bombing of airfields, nothing else.

If you have any bright ideas for settling the dispute, I, of course, would be delighted to have them. From what I am told, [newspaper columnists] Walter Lippmann and the Alsops [Stewart and Joseph] have lots of ideas, but they are far from good—about what you would expect from your youngest grandchild.

Give my love to Ibby and the family.

As ever,

1957

Eisenhower wrote to Swede briefly on November 24 and again on December 23, enclosing in the latter an invitation to attend the inauguration on January 21. Worried about Swede's increasingly poor health, he wrote that "Mamie and I would like nothing better than to have you and Ibby come to Washington for as many of the festivities as you feel able to attend, but I don't want honestly to urge you to do it since I know how tiring such a day can." By the time of the inauguration, Swede was in Bethesda Naval Hospital for treatment of the chronic high blood pressure from which he suffered. He was able, however, to attend a private swearing-in ceremony for Eisenhower's family and close friends—"except for our wedding day, it was the high point in each of our lives," Swede later wrote.

Eisenhower received regular reports on Swede's condition. "My underground sources tell me that you are getting along fine, although you have had a recurrence of those bad headaches that used to plague you," he wrote on February 20. He wrote again on March 13, shortly before his departure for a meeting with the new British prime minister, Harold Macmillan, in Bermuda.

13 March 1957

Dear Swede:

It is wretched luck that while you have been here in the hospital, I have myself been feeling so badly that I have just not had the energy to make the visit to you that I promised myself. I now understand that you are due to leave the hospital probably within a week—and of course I am delighted.

Meantime I have decided to seek the sun that so many people have recommended to me (by way of a "sea voyage" of which I am sure you will approve). So these flowers will have to take the place of the conversation I hoped we would have. They bring you my hope that those headaches will soon completely disappear and that you will really be feeling better when you get back to Chapel Hill.

With affectionate regard to you and Ibby,

As ever,

By April the situation in the Middle East had been at least temporarily resolved—the Israelis had withdrawn the last of their forces and the canal had been opened to international traffic—and Eisenhower and Macmillan, meeting in Bermuda, had restored a degree of comity to strained Anglo-American relations. At home, though he only mentions it in passing, Eisenhower was embroiled in a disorderly battle to win congressional approval of his new budget, a campaign that he handled rather ineptly and that resulted in cuts of over $4 billion. Swede, meanwhile, had been discharged from Bethesda.

Dear Swede:

I cannot tell you how much I regret that a combination of bronchitis, work, and a trip to Bermuda prevented me from coming occasionally to the hospital to see you while you were here. I truly had looked forward to an opportunity for a couple of real visits.

There is one thing that I have found out concerning the relative rank of leaders. Every time you climb a rung, you become the boss of more people but you become likewise less and less the boss of your own time. You are constantly the slave of people, events and circumstances.

Today the weather is a mere continuation of all the vile experiences we have had since mid winter. To be cold, disagreeable and rainy in Washington on April fifth is almost unbelievable but it is absolutely true.

Recently I consented (I assure you in a weak moment) again to sit for a sculptor who was determined to make a bust of me. I resent even sitting for a painter in spite of the fact that I love to see a portrait develop and I am particularly interested in the techniques a true painter uses to get the effects he sees. But to sit for a bust to my mind is about the dreariest experience a man can have and it always takes longer than does a portrait. Having learned this lesson so clearly in the past, I do not know why I again fell victim to the arguments of the artist and one or two "friends(?)."

This morning I gave the sculptor an additional half hour and as I did so I began to ponder about people, particularly the Presidents, who have undoubtedly had the same experience in the past as I am now undergoing. Friends convinced them that they "owed it to posterity" to leave a likeness in bronze or marble and they, resenting every minute of the process, consented. Now, in 1957, I looked back, as I sat in front of the sculptor, and tried to evaluate in my own mind just what those individuals actually did for this generation.

I decided that the only bust that meant much to me was the famous one of Washington. Statues and busts of Lincoln were not made until after he died, if for no other reason than while he was alive he was far more vilified than admired. While here and there I have seen busts of other Presidents—even including a head of Truman—there is no single one of them that has ever provided me with any feeling of satisfaction, much less inspiration. All of which convinces me that again I have sworn off sitting for sculptors for ever and ever, amen! So if in the future I ever write to you a new complaint on this score, please remind me that I am a weak, vacillating and easily swayed individual.

The Mid East continues to be the central factor in my thinking, in spite of the fact that the newspapers are trying to make the budget the most important item in the world today. If we could ever get a concession from Egypt that could to some degree satisfy Britain, France and Israel, I think I could regain what many people once regarded as a cheerful disposition.

The Bermuda Conference was very interesting and some day, when I have an hour or two completely to myself, I will try to give you an account of it. Macmillan is, of course, one of my intimate wartime friends and so it is very easy to talk to him on a very frank, even blunt, basis.

Right now I am off with Mamie to the farm, to be back on Sunday afternoon. The weather, as I said, is abominable, but at least it provides a change of scenery and we love the place—both its interior and the surroundings. I have had bad luck on the weather at the farm, illustrated by the fact that although I have had a skeet range there for well over a year, I have never yet fired a shot.

Give my love to Ibby and, of course, all the best to yourself, in all of which Mamie joins.

As ever,

P.S.: Of course I do most sincerely hope that those wretched headaches of yours have disappeared and that you are feeling much more like yourself.

Swede's health continued to deteriorate. Though the stay at Bethesda succeeded in bringing his blood pressure down, the fierce headaches continued, and in late June he returned to the hospital.

Dear Swede:

At this moment you are one of the mysteries of my office. We had clandestine information to the effect that you were entering Bethesda Hospital tomorrow. Inquiry at the hospital brings a report "We know nothing about it," so I will send this note to Chapel Hill in the hope that it will run you down somewhere along the line.

I am just about to take off for Williamsburg where I am to address the Conference of Governors. I have a very banal and colorless talk to deliver. While it expresses an obvious truth—that governors ought to concern themselves more with retaining states' responsibilities if they are to retain states' rights—this subject has been so often discussed that I feel like I am giving a lecture on the virtues of sunlight. Some of these speaking engagements become mere ordeals.

Of course if you are on the way here to the hospital, my office will know it before I get back and will probably have there a word of welcome to you.

I suppose it is those damnable headaches that are your present difficulty because you told me that your blood pressure situation was much improved.

These days find me riding the governmental merry-go-round at a dizzy pace. Abroad there are several problems that are immensely acute; for example Jordan, disarmament efforts, Russian propaganda, and the Korean situation.

At home, particularly here in Washington, the Budget governs the thinking, talking and action of almost every individual. Demagogues are having a field day with their particular venom being directed at "tight" money. This of course is one of the prices of prosperity. There is seemingly a much greater demand for money with which to expand than there is money.

Some people doubt that it is possible for a free government to live too long with continued prosperity. It looks as if we are having a chance to prove or disprove the charge. Possibly nations have some of the characteristics of the individual, and we know many individuals who stand poverty with good grace grow insufferable, and degenerate in character, the moment they experience any good fortune.

Enough of all this—one of these days I will try to write a letter characterized by a bit more coherence and good sense.

Give my love to Ibby, and all the best to yourself.

As ever,

6/25/57

P.S.: Immediately after I left for Williamsburg, my secretary discovered that you had indeed been admitted to Bethesda. Following my previous instructions, she sent you a few flowers and this note, of course, I shall now have delivered there. Captain [Dale J.] Crittenberger will keep in touch with your doctors and report to me. I do hope this time the doctors will find the cause of your difficulty.

By the summer of 1957, Eisenhower was engaged in a series of battles with congressional conservatives over the U.S. Status of Forces agreements and over foreign aid. The controversy over the Status of Forces agreements was precipitated by an incident in which an American soldier shot and killed a Japanese woman and was subsequently surrendered to Japanese authorities for trial. There was a move in Congress to revise all Status of Forces agreements so as to bar foreign criminal jurisdiction over United States military personnel, a move that was quickly squelched by Eisenhower's strong opposition.

He was less successful, however, in winning support for increased foreign aid. Although Congress had endorsed his call for a policy of economic and military aid to counter "Communist aggression" in the Middle East—the so-called Eisenhower Doctrine—it nevertheless slashed his requests for such aid by more than a billion dollars.

The growth of the civil-rights movement clearly troubled Eisenhower, to whom order and public tranquility were extremely important. Relatively insensitive to the plight of black Americans, he feared the passions that civil rights aroused among both blacks and white southerners. He believed that the decision in *Brown* vs. *Board of Education of Topeka, Kansas*, had been a mistake, and he refused to endorse it or to identify himself with the goal of desegregation. In his State of the Union address in January he had called for passage of a modest civil-rights bill. Though the bill was further weakened by Congress, it finally passed in August. The first civil-rights legislation in nearly a century, it established the federal Civil Rights Commission and strengthened, if only slightly, federal protection for voting rights.

Finally, he could not abide the disorderly processes of congressional politics. Congress was a warren of greedy special interests, he believed, and most congressmen were little better than demagogues. "We can't let just a popular majority sweep us in one direction," he wrote to Vice-President Nixon, "because then you can't recover." His faith in the Supreme Court was based, not on its particular decisions, with which he frequently disagreed, but on its role in providing "stability in a form of government where political expediency might at times carry parties and political leaders to extremes."

---

22 July 1957

PERSONAL

Dear Swede:

The fact that you had to remain in the hospital such a short time encourages me to believe that your condition must have improved definitely and rapidly. While I had hoped to get out to Bethesda some time when Ibby would be present, I am still delighted that you are not compelled to spend most of the summer in a hospital room.

Concerning my present situation, I think it is best described by merely saying "the grind goes on." I am repeatedly astonished, even astounded, by the apparent ignorance of members of Congress in the general subject of our foreign affairs and relationships. I realize that by this time I should accept, as a matter of course, Congressional reaction that seemingly reflects either this abysmal ignorance or a far greater concern for local political sentiment than for the welfare of the United States.

I am sure that this second possibility is *not* correct so far as the conscious attitude of the average Congressman is concerned. In the general case each of them thinks of himself as intensely patriotic; but it does not take the average member long to conclude that his first duty to his country is to get himself re-elected. This subconscious conviction leads to a capacity for rationalization that is almost unbelievable.

In any event, right at this moment lack of understanding of America's international position and obligation accounts for the fact that we seem to be trying to make a national hero out of a man who shot a woman—in the back at something like ten to fifteen yards distance.

As quickly as this incident became a popular one in some parts of the isolationist press, it was taken up by dozens of Congressmen who "viewed with alarm" and were "shocked and distressed" at the injustice done to this great soldier and citizen.

We have even had a serious attempt made to force me to denounce our Status of Forces treaties. These treaties, as you know, are fair and just to Americans serving abroad and are the only means by which we retain jurisdiction in most offenses committed. Because they establish a reasonable jurisdictional balance between ourselves and the host country, they are at the very foundation of our defensive alliances. To denounce them would make us completely isolationist and force us to abandon practically every base we have abroad.

Of course there are people who believe that the United States would not only be secure but would greatly prosper by withdrawing into a fanciful "Fortress America." I say fanciful for the reason that any sensible man knows that there can be no such thing as security in isolation, no matter if our armed forces were multiplied three-fold.

This same unreasoning attitude is reflected in the constantly repeated effort in Congress to slash mutual security funds. Again and again I have explained to individuals and to the public that, as of this moment, our mutual security operations represent America's best investment. Through them we are able to keep down the direct costs of our own military establishment. More than this, we are increasing the consuming power of many friendly nations and helping to build up future markets for our rapidly expanding productive capacity.

Last year our excess of exported goods over imported goods was something on the order of nine billion dollars. Subtract from this all of the funds that we currently send out to aid the military establishments and economies of our friends and we still have a comfortable surplus. It is quite clear that except for the funds we have spent in the past in order to give help to economies in Europe and in Asia, there would not be the purchasing power in a number of countries to buy from us.

Some people worry that the long range competitive position of the United States will be damaged if we help now to build up the productive capacity of others. Some day this might be a problem. But there are two main points to remember.

(a). If other countries improve industrially their standards of living will usually go up. This means that in the normal case their wage scales will begin to rise and eventually will come closer and closer to our own. Consequently we will still have the competitive advantage of our deeper experience in management, production and, we like to think, in inventiveness and imagination. In the meantime we will have expanding markets.

While you may argue that, in the case of Japan, increasing industrialization has raised living standards very slowly indeed, I think that as of today labor would be in a far better position in that country if their society had been a free one rather than a dictatorship.

(b). Before any of the underdeveloped countries can reach a position where they can export to others, on a competitive basis with the United States, many years must elapse and during that period their purchasing power will multiply rapidly. We, if we are wise, will share prominently in that increasing market. This applies to all of South America, Africa, and to portions of Asia, particularly in the Mid East.

All this, of course, is nothing but a by-product of a process which has as its principal purpose the strengthening of freedom and the gradual exhaustion of Communism in the world. I merely refer to it to express my belief that both in the short term and in the long term our mutual security program will advance our country's best interests.

Undoubtedly I have written to you a number of times on the subject of "Civil Rights." I think that no other single event has so disturbed the domestic scene in many years as did the Supreme Court's decision of 1954 in the school segregation case. That decision and similar ones earlier and later in point of time have interpreted the Constitution in such fashion as to put heavier responsibilities than before on the Federal government in the matter of assuring to each citizen his guaranteed Constitutional rights. My approach to the many problems has been dictated by several obvious truths:

(a). Laws are rarely effective unless they represent the will of the majority. In our prohibition experiment, we even saw local opinion openly and successfully defy Federal authority even though national public opinion then seemed to support the whole theory of prohibition.

(b). When emotions are deeply stirred, logic and reason must operate gradually and with consideration for human feelings or we will have a resultant disaster rather than human advancement.

(c). School segregation itself was, according to the Supreme Court decision of 1896, completely Constitutional until the reversal of that decision was accomplished in 1954. The decision of 1896 gave a cloak of legality to segregation in all its forms. As a result, the social, economic and political patterns of the South were considered by most whites, especially by those in that region, as not only respectable but completely legal and ethical.

(d). After three score years of living under these patterns, it was impossible to expect complete and instant reversal of conduct by mere decision of the Supreme Court. The Court itself recognized this and provided a plan for the desegration of schools which it believed to be moderate but effective.

The plan of the Supreme Court to accomplish integration gradually and sensibly seems to me to provide the only possible answer if we are to consider on the one hand the customs and fears of a great section of our population, and on the other the binding effect that Supreme Court decisions must have on all of us if our form of government is to survive and prosper. Consequently the plan that I have advanced for Congressional consideration on this touchy matter was conceived in the thought that only moderation in legal compulsions, accompanied by a stepped-up program of education, could bring about the result that every loyal American should seek.

I think that some of the language used in the attempt to translate my basic purposes into legislative provisions has probably been too broad. Certainly it has been subject to varying interpretations. This I think can be corrected in Congress.

But I hold to the basic purpose. There must be respect for the Constitution—which means the Supreme Court's interpretation of the Constitution—or we shall have chaos. We cannot possibly imagine a successful form of government in which every individual citizen would have the right to interpret the Constitution according to his own convictions, beliefs and prejudices. Chaos would develop. This I believe with all my heart—and shall always act accordingly.

This particular quarrel is not completely devoid of some amusing aspects. For example, a violent exponent of the segregation doctrine was in my office one day. During the course of his visit he delivered an impassioned talk on the sanctity of the 1896 decision by the Supreme Court. At a pause in his oration I merely asked, "Then why is the 1954 decision not equally sacrosanct?" He stuttered and said, "There were then wise men on the Court. Now we have politicians." I replied, "Can you name one man on the 1896 Court who made the decision?" He just looked at me in consternation and the subject was dropped.

I suppose at the moment a problem of possibly even greater importance to us is the threat of inflation. Indeed it has passed the point of mere threat, as evidenced by the fact that in the last year we have had about a four percent rise in living costs. Since we had in the first three and a half years of this Administration succeeded in holding this rise to under one percent, the present situation shows that accumulated pressures are at last forcing prices up—or if you want to put it another way, the dollar down.

There are so many contributory causes to inflation that it seems to be idle to pick out any one as the real culprit. Nevertheless many people try to do this. One man will wail about the wage-price spiral. Another lays everything to government spending. Still another will blame unlimited consumer credit, while others find banking policies to be wholly to blame.

Actually all these factors and even more enter into the problem. Even worse, not everybody acts consistently. Again consider the Congress. Suddenly convinced that governmental expenditures were too high—which they are—Congress entered upon a great economy drive. This it did under the belief that this subject would remain popular for so long that no better record could be taken to the voter in the fall of 1958 than one of consistent voting against expenditures.

This drive was underway long enough to provide opportunity for speeches by almost every individual member of the Congress, but by the time the first round was over, some of the boys began to wake up to the fact that a good many pressure groups wanted to dig a little deeper into the Federal treasury. As a result, in the field of housing Congress insisted upon putting a billion dollars more in the authorization bill than the Administration had requested. On top of that, Congress is in the process of passing a pay raise for mailmen that will give them a twelve percent increase even though Congress is well aware of the fact that this will practically compel raises for the entire classified civil service. This vastly increases Federal expenditures. Worse than this, there can be little doubt that the industrial wage-price spiral would get a terrific upward jolt from any such action on the part of the Federal government. But in voting as he does the Congressman feels that he is winning votes for himself. So out the window goes his concern about the effect of government expenditures on inflation.

In the same way, I doubt that there is any Congressman who fails to realize that so-called cheap money likewise has a stimulating effect on inflation. Yet he is willing to expose the country to the ravages of inflation so long as he can make a showing that he is for "cheap money for the little fellow."

I know that you will understand I am not criticizing all Congressmen. I am talking mainly about those who strive for the headlines by reckless and impulsive statements. Indeed in the normal case the average Congressman, when met individually, seems to be a perfectly logical and high-minded individual. It is usually when he gets to operating in the mass with opportunities for making rash and unwise statements that we gain such a bad impression of his capabilities.

*   *   *

This letter is far too long—you will be worn out with its reading. In any event, when I started my chief purpose was merely to express the great hope that you were improving as rapidly as your short stay in the hospital seemed to indicate you would. Everything between this paragraph and the beginning represents only the meandering reflections of an individual who has daily to use up more than a normal ration of his sense of humor in order to keep right side up. Possibly I am something like a ship which, buffeted and pounded by wind and wave, is still afloat and manages in spite of frequent tacks and turnings to stay generally along its plotted course and continues to make some, even if slow and painful, headway.

Give my love to Ibby and, as always, the best to yourself.

As ever,

Tunisia, where independence leader Habib Bourguiba presided over a former French colony, was among the least of Eisenhower's worries in the fall of 1957, despite the space he devotes to it in this letter. Far more pressing were inflation, continuing turmoil in the Middle East, the Soviet launch of an intercontinental ballistic missile, renewed pressure for a build-up at home, and, finally, the crisis over school desegregation in Little Rock, Arkansas. In Little Rock, where integration of the high school had just begun, Governor Orval Faubus had ordered in the Arkansas National Guard, ostensibly to preserve the peace but in fact to block black children from entering the school. When efforts at compromise with Faubus had failed, and after angry white mobs had driven black children from the school, Eisenhower finally and reluctantly ordered federal troops into Little Rock.

Swede, meanwhile, grew worse, struggling with increased difficulty to sustain his end of the correspondence, abandoning altogether his "Royal Ike," and writing slowly and laboriously by hand.

---

18 November 1957

PERSONAL

Dear Swede:

It is too bad that your condition of weakness does not respond more readily to treatment. If the writing of a full letter seems to become too much of a burden, why don't you, from time to time, just jot down a note, in a few words, about anything that occurs to you. When you get a package of them, send them on to me. I do think you should not waste your strength trying to compose a coherent letter—much as I like your communications.

Since July 25th of 1956, when Nasser announced the nationalization of the Suez, I cannot remember a day that has not brought its major or minor crisis. Some of these have been handled in secret; that is, no explanation or recitation of fact is possible for the simple reason that to bring some of them out in the open would cause as much trouble as the wrong answer. For example, had we published an account of the long, patient and hard work we did with the British and French, as well as the Israelis, in order to prevent the attack on Egypt and in making plain what would be our attitude in the event that such an attack was undertaken, there would have been the greatest political trouble in Britain, and probably in France. So we just had to let people think that we acted on the spur of the moment and astonished our friends by taking the action we did. Actually, they knew exactly what we'd do.

In the matters that currently seem to be disturbing the country so much, namely our relative position with Russia in arms development, you can understand that there are many things that I don't dare to allude to publicly, yet some of them would do much to allay the fears of our own people.

The most recent difficulty in the foreign field of which you have read involves our shipment of token arms to Tunisia. This we did in conjunction with the British after conversations with them demonstrated we were thinking in parallel lines.

What happened was this. Somewhere along about early September the Tunisians came to us saying that they simply had to have arms for internal security and some protection against border raids. We knew that the French were maintaining close ties with Tunisia and we urged the French to make a satisfactory arms deal with Tunisia, in order that the latter country would not turn to the

Soviets for help. The political leader in the country, Bourguiba, is a very fine friend of the West and the most intelligent man that I know of in the Arab world.

He became more and more insistent when he found that the French were using delaying and evasive tactics and he told us frankly that he would simply have to take the Soviet's offer which, financially, was far more favorable to him and his country than anything we could give him.

We and the British told the French that we would have to send a token shipment by November first because in our opinion we would otherwise risk the loss of that important area. You do not even have to glance at your map to know what the strategic value of the region is. The French then replied that they would make some delivery of the necessary arms to Tunisia and asked us to abstain. To this we gladly agreed, provided they would do it by November first.

When their government fell, they pointed out that there was no one there in power to take action and asked us to delay still further. This we did, much to the anguish of Bourguiba.

I have forgotten for the moment exactly how we fixed the date, but we then stated that we would wait until November twelfth, but we told both the French and Tunisians that, on that date, we would deliver a token shipment of arms (from us only 500 rifles). When November twelfth came, the [Félix] Gaillard government was in power but the matter had not been settled., Under our pressing, the French government *finally* said it intended to deliver the arms and had agreed in principle to do so, but before actual delivery could take place *the Tunisians would have to agree that their whole source of arms supply from then on would be France.*

In other words, even though Tunisia is ostensibly a free government, one with which we have exchanged Ambassadors, the French asked them to agree that for any military purposes they would be completely subservient to the French.

As you might expect, Bourguiba flatly rejected this condition and insisted that we deliver the token shipment of arms, as promised.

On our part, we felt it was a matter of good faith to deliver on November twelfth, but since the French seemed at last to be aware of the grim seriousness of the situation, we put off, with the British, actual delivery for another twenty-four to forty-eight hours, to give the French a renewed chance to settle the matter.

[The next nine lines are still classified, in accordance with restrictions imposed by the Eisenhower family in their deed of gift.]

In spite of our actions, taken with the utmost caution and after long and exhaustive conferences, to postpone delivery after November twelfth, and so again breaking a promise we had given in good faith, the French went back to the Tunisians with the same old argument—namely that they, the French, had to be the sole source of supply of arms for Tunisia.

With the matter in this highly unsatisfactory state, we finally delivered the token shipment on November fourteenth, and France has since been acting like a spoiled child.

Of course we were well aware that France was seeking any kind of excuse to blame someone else for its own difficulties. That is a favorite trick of French politicians these days. But no matter how serious the consequences, we decided that if we were to hold on to the Mid East and have any kind of decent relations with the Arab world, we simply had to go ahead with an agreement that seemed to us to be based on Tunisian rights and on fairness in our dealings with other nations.

Just what the outcome will be I cannot say. The French are fully capable of the most senseless action just to express their disagreement with others.

Their basic trouble is that they are still trying to act as if they headed a great empire, all of it, as of old, completely dependent on them. If they would center their attention mainly on their European problems and work with others in their solution, they could be a happy and prosperous country.

Today their production per man is, I am told by the experts, even higher than that in Germany. Yet Germany is making money hand over fist, and France is on the verge of bankruptcy.

* * *

I am slated to make two or three more speeches this fall, or at least by the end of January. Subjects still to be covered are such things as "The function of mutual security assistance in our nation's defense," "The farm problem," and the "Economic situation." This last I will defer for some time because of the hope that a few of the uncertainties will be cleared up and I can make a more meaningful talk on the matter.

You mention the Little Rock situation and your conviction that I had done the right thing. My biggest problem has been to make people see, particularly in the south, that my main interest is not in the integration or segregation question. My opinion as to the wisdom of the decision or the timeliness of the Supreme Court's decision has nothing to do with the case.

The point is that specific orders of our Courts, taken in accordance with the terms of our Constitution as interpreted by the Supreme Court, must be upheld.

I said to a man the other day: "You disagree with the decision and tell me that I should show my disapproval by refusing to prevent violence from obstructing the carrying-out of the Court's orders."

"Let us take a different example. Suppose you had been thrown into jail by an arbitrary sheriff or United States marshal. Your lawyer asked for a writ of habeas corpus and it is granted by the judge. But the feeling in the locality is such that the sheriff feels completely safe in telling you he will not obey the order, and you will remain in jail. Now comes my question: Would you consider I was doing my solemn duty as the President of the United States if I did not compel your release from jail?"

If the day comes when we can obey the orders of our Courts only when we personally approve of them, the end of the American system, as we know it, will not be far off.

Along with these speaking chores that I mentioned a while back, I have the State of the Union speech to make, a Budget in preparation to send to Congress, the Economic Report to approve and send on, and then the endless conferences with legislative leaders while Congress is in session. The only hope I see for any real letup is some time around next July. Several things would have to happen to make that period any better than the present.

The Congress would have to adjourn early. There would have to be a general easing off of tensions in the free world. And fewer people must be struggling to see me with "very important messages and pieces of advice." If all three of these things happen, possibly my family, my associates, my secretary and I can give less attention to our blood pressure and the condition of our general nervous systems.

Having said all this, I must tell you that physically I seem to stand up under the burden remarkably well. Yesterday I think the doctor said my blood pressure was 130 over 80 and my pulse something on the order of 66.

The biggest worry of all is the constant question of "doing the right thing." Certain of the problems are so complex and so difficult that there is no really satisfactory answer. As [John] Foster [Dulles] explained it the other day when we were talking about the French-Tunisian mess, "This is a matter of choosing whether you want your arm broken in two places—or your leg broken above the knee." But I have the satisfaction of knowing that I do my best, that I have with me a group of honest, dedicated, and in some cases very wise men to advise and help, and that, finally, the Almighty must have in mind some better fate for this poor old world of ours than to see it largely blown up in a holocaust of nuclear bombs.

So with this kind of support I manage to keep at least the shreds of a once fairly good disposition—a matter on which Mrs. Whitman may write you a minority report—and all in all feel that the job is being done about as well as it can be under the circumstances.

While I am often urged to be more assertive, to do a little more desk-pounding, to challenge Russia more specifically and harshly, I do not do these things for the simple reason that I think they are unwise. Possibly I do not always control my temper well, but I do succeed in controlling it in public. And I still believe that a frequent exhibition of a loss of temper is a sure sign of weakness.

I seem to have gotten into a spate of introspective thinking here and making you the victim of its expression. Actually I have nothing quite so important to do as to wish for you a reasonable and quick return to a state of good feeling, particularly in getting rid of those blankety-blankety headaches. Along with this, I want to send my love to Ibby and your family.

As ever,

On November 25, while at his desk, Eisenhower suffered a stroke that left him briefly paralyzed and unable to speak coherently. As word of the stroke spread through Washington, there were rumors of resignation and calls, in Congress and by the press, for the president to step down. Even Eisenhower was heard to mumble that "if I cannot attend to my duties, I am simply going to give up this job." But as with his earlier illnesses, Eisenhower's powerful will and strong constitution once again took over; and by the time his secretary, Ann Whitman, wrote the following letter to Swede, Eisenhower was already recovering.

1 December 1957

PERSONAL

Dear Captain Hazlett:

All week I have wanted to write you this note, not that I can add anything to the news I know you get daily about the President, but to try to reassure you—and myself at the same time—that the President is really going to be all right again. Incidentally, just in case you didn't see it, I am enclosing a copy of an editorial in the New York Times of yesterday that has touched me more than anything else these last difficult days.

You remember, of course, the President's letter from Augusta. Now that I think back I could have offered a minority report. I only knew then that I was fighting a losing battle against the pace that the President seemingly had compulsively set for himself. We had all ignored those hard lessons of the heart attack aftermath and everybody seemed to be dumping all the unsolvable problems squarely in his lap. With the Sputniks and Little Rock and the failures of the last Congress still fresh, there wasn't ever for the President, here in Washington at least, a moment that he could use to think. He was, furthermore, wrestling with speeches at all hours of day and night, and under great pressure. For instance, a concrete example of what I mean was the Oklahoma speech. I had no plans to go on that trip, but at noon that day the speech was still far from final. So typewriters were dumped on the plane and somehow or other we finished it. All that tends to build up in me and must for the President be magnified a thousand times, a tenseness that means loss of sleep, and a feeling always that you are not doing the job right because there simply isn't time.

On the plus side, I think the high government officials and the President's staff have learned, this time, that they must stand on their own feet. I believe the President is the only person who can save the world today for a future that surely could be bright. If we can un-clutter his desk with the trivia (and I take that back, it really isn't trivia) but the less of the more important, I think he is the only person who can weld our friends into a cohesive group and overcome the suspicions of our potential enemies. And certainly he has the courage and will to do his best, despite all these blows that fate throws him.

I seem to have wandered far from what I meant to be a reassuring note to you. I know how worried you are. These are little simple things: The President has called me on the phone several times since last Monday. He has seemed absolutely perfect in his speech. There is positively no loss of anything except this business of trying to find the right word, and that occurs only when he is tired. One of his friends from New York saw him yesterday at the farm, and reported that he looked just fine.

We had an alert out at Bethesda, but apparently you did not go there for the overnight checkup that you wrote the President [about]. Please let us know if you go through Washington, if only so that Captain Crittenberger or I can bring you fully up to date on the President.

Don't think of answering this; it does me good to write to someone as close as you are to the President. And please forgive my bad (Sunday, let's call it) typing.

Sincerely,

[Ann C. Whitman]

P.S. Couldn't you have been generous and let Army (and the President) win yesterday?

1958

In December, Swede began a long handwritten letter to Eisenhower, a letter that, given Swede's faltering health and the continued interruption of savage headaches, took him more than a month to complete. Ann Whitman typed it up for the president, who scrawled his own reactions on the margins. In his letter, Swede expressed his admiration for Eisenhower's determination to attend the NATO Conference, "in a wheel chair if necessary"; praised Secretary of State Dulles, Assistant to the President Sherman Adams, and Secretary of Agriculture Ezra Taft Benson; criticized actor and television advisor Robert Montgomery's staging of Eisenhower's television address on his return from Paris ("to be frank, you looked decidedly ill at ease"); and applauded Eisenhower's selection of Neil H. McElroy as secretary of defense. "I'm afraid, though, that you can't expect too much enthusiasm on his part as regards further tightening of the bonds of service integration. As you undoubtedly know, he ran [Procter and Gamble] on the theory of inter-departmental rivalries." Swede attacked columnist Drew Pearson, who in a television interview had predicted that, within a year, Eisenhower would no longer be president; criticized French actions in Tunisia; and on the proposed Summit meeting with the Russians, concluded that "unless the prospects show a real promise of concrete achievement I think you would be wasting your time." "I agree fully," wrote Eisenhower in the margin.

In late February, Eisenhower wrote the following "birthday" letter to Swede.

Dear Swede:

Since I want both to send you felicitations for that non-existent birthday of yours and to answer, at least briefly, some of the comments in your most recent letter (which I enjoyed tremendously, as I always do), I shall try to limit myself to those subjects you bring up and not go off on my usual lengthy, and I like to think philosophical, discourse.

Now as to your points. Please don't concern yourself about any lack of coherence, if such there ever might be, in your letters. The important thing is that you don't tire yourself in writing them. I always like to have your thoughts, and they don't have to be in any logical order for them to be of value to me.

As for my recent physical mishap, never at any time did I feel *ill*, so I don't deserve any special commendation for making the Paris trip. My only apprehension was about the formal speeches I knew I would have to make, and, to some extent, concerning the informal conferences with the various heads of government. But all in all, the experience was pleasant and I think all to the good. I especially got a kick out of my visit to my old SHAPE Headquarters.

With reference to the illness itself, apparently months will be needed to complete the full cure. But the only symptom I notice now is a tendency to use the wrong word—for example, I may say "desk" when I mean "chair." But that tendency seems to be decreasing and people who haven't seen me for months say, honestly I think, that they notice a much improved condition in this ailment.

You know how I feel about the Secretary of State, both from previous letters and from the many public statements I have made. I admire tremendously his wisdom, his knowledge in the delicate and intricate field of foreign relations, and his tireless dedication to duty. Apparently with strangers his personality may not always be winning, but with his friends he is charming and delightful. In addition to Mr. Dulles, Secretary Benson and Governor Adams are two individuals who have been, in my opinion, unjustly attacked. They are also dedicated and completely honest men. But in this business sometimes glibness gives more surface reward than does honesty.

Speaking of personalities, the new Russian Ambassador to the United States, Mr. Mikhail Menshikov, is making quite a splash in Washington. He is extremely affable, good-looking (I am told by the ladies of my family) in the "Western sort of way" (whatever they mean by that), energetic and apparently not impressed with protocol procedures (which break with routine I admit I find refreshing). Only time will tell whether his appointment is in any way indicative of a change in official Russian policy.

Oh yes, I agree completely that Bob Montgomery erred in his "stage directions" for the report to the nation immediately after the NATO Conference.

Now to go back to your letter and to my health. I am trying to follow the advice of the doctors. I want to keep well and conserve my energy as much as possible for the tasks that lie ahead of me. But it is not easy since politicians have a habit of making me ill—mentally and physically! I cannot, for example, understand why any one, Democrat or Republican, would want to fan the flames of the so-called "recession" for his own political advantage at the expense of all Americans. But you know as well as I do that such a thing is done daily for the cheap advantage that certain people feel they will gain personally. In the same category I put the request of some thirty Congressmen that I "fire" Benson simply because they are so avid for more governmental handouts for the farmers in their districts.

Already we are in the special fever of a campaign year. If a Republican Congress could be elected it would be the neatest trick of the week. The brickbats that will be thrown at me I shall ignore, and I shall concentrate, as I have tried to do in the past, upon our national security, upon inching toward a just and durable peace for all the world, and upon sustaining the health of the American economy.

Secretary McElroy is, in my opinion, one of the best appointments that could be made. He may have started out, as you say, without too much enthusiasm for service integration, but I think he is changing his views. He has, incidentally, absorbed with unexpected rapidity the enormous complexity of the Defense Department and will, I think, make a tremendous contribution there.

This whole business of inter-service rivalries has been greatly distressing to me, and to all of us. I am sure you are as sick as I am of public debates among Generals and the Secretaries of the various services. You referred to the German General staff system.

I venture that few people really understand what happened under that so-called system. Their General Staff was *Army.** For that it was superb. But military separation in compartments was marked. Even the Ministry of War in 1914 had nothing to do with the General Staff.

I have had endless discussions in my office on the relative merits of the nuclear submarines versus nuclear aircraft carriers. I agree with you completely that the flattop is becoming obsolete and I have tried, and will continue to try, to convince the Navy big brass that their only possible use would be in a *small* war. Here you get down to an *intra* service rivalry that presents its problems, too.

As for the columnist [Drew Pearson] you mention, I merely say that I have not read a word of his in fifteen years. Personally I think he is a "spherical" SOB which makes him one no matter from what angle you may view him. And as for the prophecy you mention, I had not heard of it before. He *could* of course be right. But I think the good Lord will have more to do with what happens than this particular columnist.

You bring up the fact that retired officers are not included in the Administration's recommendations for "cost of living" increases. These recommendations were based on the Cordiner report, which was designed to keep in the services young, able officers and *real* technicians. While the Cordiner report provided for very large increases in senior grades, the theory was that this would keep young officers in the service permanently. The general policy was to ignore all others. (This report was made, of course, when inflation was our number one domestic problem.) I think we might review the matter now, and I am assured by the experts that, in any event, the Congress will, for its own political reasons, see that retired personnel are included when the issue is finally decided.

I mentioned briefly the "recession" that is worrying everyone today. We are watching the economy closely and I still believe, as I said in my last press conference, that there will be more employment opportunities by mid- or late March. But this may mark the "beginning of the end" of the recession; it will be quite a while before we reach the "end of the ending." I shall never approve a tax cut for political reasons, but there are certain economists who believe that *if the recession continues*, we may have to give serious consideration to the possibility.

And a few brief points—I agree with you completely with regard to Bourguiba and I deplore the situation the French have gotten themselves, and indirectly us, into. [Félix] Gaillard [premier of France] is inexperienced (though in this specific instance I do not believe he was to blame) but basically he seems to have some of the marks of a capable leader.

Now we come to the Summit Conference. If we and our allies can first agree on the positions we will take on the various subjects that will be discussed; if the Russians will agree to a preparatory conference at a lower level; and if they will promise to abide by the agreements made at the preparatory conference—then, and only then, I am willing to meet with them. If this procedure is followed, I think we can at least hope for some success; anything else is bound to bring dismal failure.

I think I have covered all your comments except the most important ones—the fine Navy football game of last year, your health, and your birthday anniversary. I was proud of Navy's team (except on one day that need not be mentioned) and I watched them on TV whenever I could.

As you know without my telling you, I am distressed about the seeming lack of progress in your physical condition and I keep hoping that the doctors will find something that will make you more comfortable. I am glad you have decided to come back to Bethesda for another go-round and I shall keep praying that the doctors there will come up with something that will help you.

And now you are about to have a birthday anniversary, an event that I suspect you regard with as much dislike and disdain as I do. But at least you have to endure only fifteen or sixteen actual such days, while I have that imposing sixty-seven always to contemplate. But I fancy even that is little enough comfort in view of falling chests, hair and energy. At any rate you know that my prayer is that your birthday "present" for the next year will be better health.

With affectionate regard to Ibby and all the best to yourself,

As ever,

P.S.: Please let me know when you come to Bethesda; otherwise, I shall have to employ my special intelligence system.

* I am referring here to the justly famous General Staff of 1914. Of course under Hitler there was a personal Chief of Staff that could

presumably issue orders to any service. Actually Goering, as long as he was in favor, went his own way. [This note was apparently added at a later date.]

Eisenhower soon recovered from the mild stroke that he had suffered. Swede's health, however, continued to fail, and in March he returned once more to Bethesda for further tests.

---

25 March 1958

Dear Swede:

I understand from my private intelligence system that you are still undergoing tests out at Bethesda. I know you realize how strongly I pray that medical science will finally find the answer to your difficulty and some way to alleviate it.

Over the weekend, as perhaps you know, I went to Augusta in search of the elusive sun and a decent game of golf. The sun I found but there was absolutely no consolation in the brand of game I exhibited.

Perhaps these flowers will be a spot of color in your room; at the very least they will assure you that I am thinking of you.

With warm regard,

As ever,

In April the doctors at Bethesda discovered that Swede had cancer and operated, removing his right lung. Eisenhower received regular reports on the operation and on Swede's slow recovery. In August, Swede and Ibby moved to Bethesda, Maryland, where they bought a small cottage near the hospital. Here Swede began the last letter that he would attempt to write. "He struggled so hard to write to you," wrote Ibby, who later sent it to Eisenhower. "He wanted very much to thank you for all that you had done for him." In October, Swede was again hospitalized with a recurrence of the cancer. "His courage is magnificent," wrote Ibby. "I don't know how he bears such continual pain. I just hope and pray that we both will be given the strength that we need to face what lies ahead."

---

23 October 1958

Dear Ibby:

Your note about my birthday anniversary, together with the letter Swede had struggled so valiantly to write me the latter part of August, reached me this morning on the last leg of my West Coast jaunt. I am, of course, grateful for your felicitations and good wishes.

I have, of course, gotten regular reports on Swede. His courage I have always admired, and I know he faces this battle with his flags flying.

You might tell Swede, if possible, that when I was in Abilene everyone asked about him. The town looks much the same. I saw Maud Hurd briefly; as you probably know she is not at all well but she is as keen and alert as ever. Charlie Case is unchanged by the years and as great a fan of Swede's as ever.

If there is anything I can do for you, please do not fail to let me know. I would like to see you (although I don't know how or when), but from the medical reports I have had, I don't believe I should try to see Swede. He understands, I am sure, that he is constantly in my thoughts and prayers.

With warm regards,

Affectionately,

Swede's funeral at Arlington National Cemetery, 5 November 1958 (National Park Service photograph, courtesy of Dwight D. Eisenhower Library).

At the end of October, Swede died and was buried in Arlington National Cementery. Eisenhower, who was present at the funeral, sent Ibby the following note.

November 1958

Dear Ibby:

This note is simply to say what of course you already know. The prayers and hearts of Mamie and myself are with you today, as they have been in the past; we are thinking of you and all the members of your family with love and devotion.

I can never quite tell you what Swede meant to me. While I am glad for his sake that he suffers no longer, his passing leaves a permanent void in my life.

Affectionately,

Index

210